Encountering the Kingdom

Acknowledgements

I want to thank you, Jesus.
Without you, my life would be empty and void,
but your voice pierced the darkness in which I dwelled
and created a wonderful light.

I also want to thank you for my loving
and supportive wife, Geralynn;
without her I could have never experienced
your love here on earth.
Thank you for my children;
Joshua, the prophetic and sensitive one
Cody, the evangelistic and excited one
Katelynn, my determined miracle child and
Aubrey, the restorer of my joy.

Thank you for Mom and Bill who taught me love and
my entire family who taught me friendship.

Thank you for Dad and Carol who taught me
how truly restoring your love is.

Thank you for Bishop, because even when you took
Dad home, you never left me fatherless.

Finally thank you for everyone who supported me in this
project through whatever small help they may have provided.
(Brian, Willis, Brad, Kristen, Duvale, Jennie, David, Wendy
and anyone else I may have forgotten.)

Encountering the Kingdom

A Diary of Discovery

David J Jackson

A Winding Road Ministries Publication

ENCOUNTERING THE KINGDOM

A Winding Road Ministries Publication

Requests or information regarding *Encountering the Kingdom* or David J Jackson should be address to:

www.windingroadministries.com

Cover: Joshua Holnagel

Editing: Geralynn Jackson and Brad Beals @ Versitext Editing

Printed in the United States of America

ISBN 978-0-578-02200-0

Ten suggestions for maximizing this book's potential

Below are ten suggestions, not "commandments", to help you maximize the ideas presented in this book.

1. <u>Underline, highlight or mark every entry that grabs your attention</u>. Every time you emphasize something you increase your ability to retain that information because your attention is focused.

2. <u>Read only one or two chapters at a setting</u>. The human mind can only absorb so much information at one setting. Take your time and enjoy the material.

3. <u>Scan what you underlined in the previous chapter before beginning the next one</u>. Reading your highlighted information will help you refresh your memory and allow you to connect the ideas between chapters.

4. <u>Make a decision to put the ideas presented in this book into action</u>. Good intentions are only as good as the deeds behind them. Step out and try at least three ideas presented in this book and see what happens.

5. <u>Keep a journal</u>. Write down the ideas you want to see operating in your life. You can also write down any verses that are mentioned and add your own notes.

6. <u>Share the book</u>. Tell someone about the book and what you have read. It is a proven fact that the more you repeat something the deeper it forces the information into your memory. When you are done, pass it on. Do not let it lay idle on a shelf and collect dust.

7. <u>Pray the prayers</u>. Every time you come across a prayer, pray it out loud. There is power hidden in any confession we make with our mouth.

8. <u>Read the book again in six months</u>. You can read the whole book or you can just read the parts you highlighted. Either of these will help you recall and retain the knowledge better.

9. <u>Become curious</u>. Ask yourself what you really believe about God. Be willing to accept that He is more than you ever imagined and act upon it.

10. <u>Answer every question and fill in all the blanks whenever you are asked to write something down</u>. You can then review them at a later date and see how much you have grown.

About the Author...

David Jackson resides in the Mid-Michigan area with his wife, Geralynn and their four children, Joshua, Cody, Katelynn and Aubrey. He and his wife both teach science in the public school system. After a battle with a heart attack and the loss of a child, both David and Geralynn decided to renew their search for God. In their journey they discovered something about God that changed their lives forever. In the pages that follow David shares their stories and insights of what they found.

God is still revealing Himself today in ways they could never have imagined. Together they have helped people of all ages and faiths to experience God for themselves. They believe it is each person's right to hear and know God on a personal level, so please join them in discovering an appreciation for the presence of God.

"If you hold to my teaching, you are really my disciples. Then you will know the truth, and the truth will set you free."

Jesus
John 8:31-32 NIV

Encountering the Kingdom

Foreword

In my youthful mind, I believed when life was good, then God was good. As I got older I discovered life was not as simple as I imagined. My attitudes about God changed. Blaming God for the bad situations and taking credit for the good times seemed appropriate. My hard work justified all my good fortunes, but when things were difficult and out of my control I blamed God for not getting involved and making things right. The news reported all kinds of death and despair in the world. Where was God? He should have been doing something about these terrible events, as well as, making my life easier and more rewarding.

I really do not know when I accepted this mind set, but it was gradual. Finally one day I decided to actually ask God why I thought this way. To my amazement He answered and I discovered a person I never knew; someone who actually cared about my life. Why had I not seen this before? How could I have missed such a good friend? Part of the world tried to make me believe He did not exist. Others tried to convince me He was cruel and liked to inflict punishment. How could I have been so wrong?

The purpose of this book is to let everyone know that God's very nature is goodness. His focus is to bring life to us, not pain and suffering. We are actually in a specific place and time in history where He has provided every opportunity to make Himself accessible. God has placed all of His anger and frustration with mankind completely aside. He holds nothing in His heart except love and acceptance. Complete forgiveness is hard for many of us to accept and even more difficult to trust, but if you give God the chance His friendship can become one of your greatest joys.

In the pages that follow I want to tell you about the person I met. We call him God. To me He is no longer a stranger, but a friend. He is more than I ever imagined. He is a King who allowed a simple man to walk beside Him and discover who He really is. This is my story.

David Jackson

I no longer call you servants, because a master doesn't confide in his servants. Now you are my friends, since I have told you everything the Father told me.

John 15:15 NLT

- *Chapter One* -

God Calling

"God never stops trying to get our attention."

Heart Issues

I awoke this particular morning with an annoying backache. After a short time the pain began to shoot through my chest and run down my left arm. I had been sick that week and decided to ignore the symptoms so I could keep up my busy pace. My responsibilities demanded that I continue on. Today, however, my body firmly requested I change my itinerary. The pain was severe enough to make me seek medical attention.

In the emergency room my symptoms provided me prompt attention, and when one doctor left and three returned I knew something was wrong. "*Mr. Jackson, we believe you have had a heart attack.*" This was not possible. I was only thirty two and rarely sick, hardly even a cold. The cardiologist assigned to my case ran a battery of tests over the next few days. Each test confirmed the heart attack, so I was given two choices: stay in the hospital for three weeks to strengthen, then submit to a stress test; or undergo a surgical heart catherization that day to evaluate my heart's condition. I elected the catherization because it gave immediate results, and the doctor mentioned that being released was an option if the results were satisfactory. The thought of being at home sounded wonderful.

As I lay on the operating table, the surgeon told a few jokes to keep things light. All I could muster was, *"Just give me some good news!"* His response made me understand the severity of the situation. *"Every test has revealed you had a heart attack, so I'm here to assess the damage. To find nothing wrong with your heart would imply you had what we call a false positive. That would mean your heart is fine even though every test indicated a cardiac event. To be honest, I have only seen that once before."*

I was awake during the entire process and able to watch the monitor as the dye was injected into the veins that surrounded my heart. Each time, the surgeon commented on how good things looked. After injecting the last vein he said, *"Hmm, I'll be with you in a moment,"* and walked out. He returned while I was in the recovery room and calmly stated, *"Consider this a big warning. There is nothing wrong with your heart as far as I can see. It is probably a good time to take a look at your lifestyle."* He then shook my hand and left. I had achieved the rare false positive. What a relief! I was free to go home and recuperate.

The pain in my arm came and went over the next few weeks, and my cardiologist suggested an aspirin regimen if my arm continued to bother me. I was free to call him if the pain intensified. The pain did not subside; in fact, it continued for several months. Another battery of tests cleared my heart as the culprit, and the reason for the consistent ache in my arm was never determined. Thoughts of endless youth faded and I decided to reassess my priorities. Family became more important than the pursuit of the American dream. As I spent more time playing with my boys and enjoying my wife, I realized what a precious gift my family was to me. They were no longer a burden or an obstacle to achieving my goals. They gave my life purpose.

Up to this point in my life, pursuing God was not all that important. In fact, here I was, thirty-two years old and still avoiding the topic of God. As I began to think back on all the things about God that I remembered as a boy, there was one particular situation that came to mind.

Standing Taller

As a child I contracted a bacterial bone infection, called osteomyelitis, which eventually led to the death of some bone tissue in my right leg. The mortality rate was extremely high for a two year old child in those days and when my temperature hovered near 108^0 the Doctor suggested that my mom be prepared for all possibilities. Heart broken, she called in our priest to administer last rites. Amazingly, within hours after the prayers my condition noticeably changed. And after three years of experimental operations, high doses of penicillin, and months of isolation, I pulled through.

By the time I was five I was given a clean bill of health. Being alive was wonderful, but the years of surgeries and medicines had their side affects. In fighting the disease my body had sent more nutrients to the sick leg to aid the battle and this had increased the growth rate. My right leg ended up being more than an inch longer than my left. This discrepancy in my legs also caused a curvature in my spine. All of this happened years before my parent's big conversion to God. Mom informed me that my sickness was a turning point in her life. She always believed God played a large role in my healing.

By the time I was nine we were forced to deal with the leg differences so that the curvature of my spine would not increase. I was measured for a lift that would correct the shortness in my left leg, but before the lift could be delivered we encountered our first family miracle. My parents had been attending evening meetings in our church that were supposed to be more "charismatic" than the regular Sunday morning services. After one of these meetings my father sat me down and gathered the entire family around us. Dad was convinced God could heal my legs. Once he placed my feet into his hands, the difference in my legs became quite evident to everyone. He began to pray. I do not remember the words, but I do remember vividly what we all saw that night. To the astonishment of the entire family we watched my left leg miraculously grow out and meet my right leg with equal length. Dad told me to stand up and walk around. The leg appeared normal and I had not felt a thing! We all saw it happen and there was no denying what we witnessed.

Mom scheduled an appointment with the pediatrician who had worked with us throughout the entire osteomylitis ordeal. After seeing me through numerous surgeries and years in casts, he was well aware of the problems with my legs. He asked the reason for our visit. Mom requested he measure my legs again, and with some reluctance he obliged, but he also reminded Mom that the lifts for my shoes were already ordered. There was no need to do this again. Doctor Brown measured my legs and found only a quarter-inch difference in the bone length between the two. *"This slight difference is common to most of us; our heel pads make up for the discrepancy,"* he remarked, then asked, *"David's legs are normal and I know bone length does not change that much in one week, so what happened?"* Mother told him of our remarkable experience.

> If it were not for the miracles, I would have missed God's presence.

Years later when I returned to his office with my own children, he mentioned to the nurses that I was the boy with the osteomylitis whose leg miraculously grew. By their responses it was evident they were familiar with the story.

That experience stayed with all of us throughout the years. It was the first time I had seen the true power of God at work. Even now, when my brother mentions that time my leg grew out and I just simply smile and say, *"It was awesome!"* We cannot hide from the fact that God showed up that day. My legs testify to that miracle every time I take a step. What we experienced became a permanent part of our lives.

My parents tapped into something more powerful

than any of us realized. We saw lives turned around and bodies healed without explanation. If it were not for the miracles I witnessed, I would have totally ignored Mom and Dad's trust in God. These extraordinary events made a strong impression on my life. They slowly opened my eyes to the idea that there was something more to this God stuff than I knew. My heart attack was another opportunity for God to reveal Himself. I may be a slow learner when it comes to God, but now I was more aware of His presence once again.

New Direction

Even with a clean bill of health, in the back of my mind, I still wondered if I was having other heart-related problems due to the lingering aches and pains in my arm and chest. Summer arrived and it allowed us to enjoy some welcomed relaxation. Dad and I could be found in our lawn chairs discussing life on a daily basis. Dad could see that my heart attack left me a little unnerved, so one day he pressed me on a topic we rarely discussed, and made a suggestion. *"You should give your life to the Lord and serve him!"* A year ago I would have calmly explained to him how I had my whole life planned and how smoothly everything was working out, but not that day. I had nothing to say, nowhere to run, and no more gimmicks to get me out of my current situation. I had tried every worldly avenue to make my life happy. The American dream was not solving life's problems and I knew it. Busyness and stress had taken their toll. God was one direction I had not tried, so I agreed.

The prayer was simple:

"God, forgive me for all my sins and mistakes. Take over my life and help me live the life you desire. I accept your forgiveness in Jesus' name. Amen."

Something inside me changed that day. My spiritual DNA was altered and I have never been the same since. All my senses were supercharged. Every color seemed so much richer; the sky was bluer, the grass was greener, and the clouds were a white I had never seen. I could not explain it, but the heaviness of life was gone. A new zeal overtook me within days, and I felt purpose again. A transformation had begun in me that I had never expected. Deep inside I felt different, though outwardly life was the same. There was a peace I had not felt in years. The pains were becoming distant memories. My greatest companion became the Bible, and the words seemed to have a life of their own. The change was so fast and so complete that I had to ask myself, *"Was God in the background all these years just waiting for me find Him?"* One day, to my surprise, God answered that question.

> I only took a small step of faith, but it has made all the difference.

Called Out

It was now Fall, almost a full year after my heart attack and just a few months after my internal renovation. My sister Karen invited our family to a nearby church to listen to a visiting speaker. We were looking to learn more about God, so we decided to attend. Karen informed us that this particular minister had a unique spiritual gifting. Apparently, he was able to hear from God, and he used his gifting to strengthen people who were going through tough times by giving them words of encouragement.

At first, I was a little skeptical, but people were evidently touched by the minister's words, and they seemed very genuine in their responses. It was not until he called me out of the crowd that I realized the truth of his gifting. After looking intently at me for a few moments, he said in a polite way that God had a word for me, and that I would have to judge the word for myself. He continued, *"God says your heart is totally healed. You will have no more problems the rest of your life and God wants you to know that He has something for you to do."* I was shocked because his words were right on target. There was no way he could have known about my heart or the stress that it had created, nor could he have known of my quest to discover if God was reaching out to me, since none of us had ever met him. I was convinced God had to be involved.

My wife began to cry as we both felt the stress of my heart episode lift off us. It has now been over ten years since the incident; I still visit the cardiologist, and his tests always confirm my healing. God has kept His promise and my health is a witness to His faithfulness. That day I realized God was calling me and I just needed to listen. I only took a small step of faith by asking God to get involved in my life, but it has made all the difference. I went on to experience more than I could ever have imagined, and this was just the beginning.

Task at Hand ✋

Reflect back on your life and see if you can think of a few situations where God might have been involved and write them in the space provided.

I believe God was trying to get my attention when...

_____

_____

_____

_____

_____

_____

_____

_____

_____

_____

_____

_____

_____

_____

_____

_____

_____

_____

God has focused <u>all</u> His resources on getting our attention, because His love for us demands it!

Helpful Biblical Principle

See how very much our heavenly Father loves us, for he allows us to be called his children, and we really are!

1 John 3:1 NLT

- *Chapter Two* -

Experience

"To believe in God you must experience God"

Experience

One particular moment with my children had a great impact on my relationship with God. We were sitting around the breakfast table discussing the Bible when I raised the question about doubting God's existence. I asked each of my children to give me a percentage, from one to a hundred, of how much they truly believed that God existed. My daughters, five and six at the time, were not able to give percentages, but they did respond with a strong, *"I believe in God, Dadda."* It was the answer of my sixteen year old son that made me think. He told me, *"Dad, I'm about 95%. I know God exists because too many things have happened in my life that I know only God could have done. It is doing what is right that I have a hard time with."* Wow! 95%! My son had experienced God working in his life so much that believing God existed was not difficult for him. That was unshakable faith. My other son, who was fifteen years old, honestly revealed he was at 50%. He admitted that he still struggled with believing in God. We all do at sometime in our lives.

My children's responses set my mind into motion. I posed the same question to some friends. Very few responded with percentages above 50%. When someone indicated they had a strong belief, higher than 50%, I would inquire into the reason for such faith. They were able to relate their trust to a particular event in their life which had a profound impact on their belief in God. It was at those moments they felt as if God had made Himself known. After years of asking this question I began to notice something about the people who struggle with the existence of God.

People who do not have a strong belief in God tend to fall into several categories. These are merely my observations and do not truly encompass every single person. One collection of people are those who think they have life pretty much figured out. They believe God serves no real purpose. They were probably raised in a stable home, got a form of higher education, and built a career that provides all the comforts of a successful life. They do not mind attending church, but it just does not touch their heart. If God does exist, they will get a reward because they feel they are basically good at heart. Besides, God has to be pleased with them because they are able to take care of themselves. They are the independents.

A second set are those who have faced more difficulties in life, and their hardships required them to seek help from a higher source. They tried God and found it full of empty promises. During their trials they felt that God did not answer them or fix the problem in the way they thought it should have been handled. Some of these people have heard of God's great promises, but have never seen anything materialize. Life has never improved. They harbor a grudge and believe that since God did not help, He does not exist! Whether they call themselves atheists or not, they have decided there is no purpose to looking into the idea of God any further. Sometimes even the mere mention of God sets off a flurry of bad memories. They are the scorekeepers.

The last group of people, I like to call the justifiers. These are the people who do not want to be accountable for their lifestyle or their choices. To denounce God's existence gives them the justification and an ease of conscience to maintain their way of life. Change appears too costly to them.

Being an independent, a scorekeeper, or a justifier allows us to push God to the side. We are then free to forge out a life based on our own initiatives. Can you place yourself into one of these categories? Or maybe you fall into more than one. I was mostly an independent and a scorekeeper, but I also saw myself as a justifier at times.

> My heart attack made me reopen the God chapter of my life.

During critical struggles in my life I asked God for His input, but felt He did not want to help, mostly because circumstances did not turn out as I wanted them to. So I relied on my strong will to get along without Him and did quite well for a number of years. But my heart attack made me reopen the God chapter of my life. I was in need of a tangible experience that would allow me to finally decide who

God was. My meager attempt in the past to find God was not valid proof and neither was my skeptic friends' advice. Theories were no longer good enough and I decided to give God another chance. Looking for evidence of God's existence became a priority, my goal was not to test God, but simply to be open to the possibility of His existence.

My wife and I decided we were going to give God as many chances as we could to reveal Himself, and we did this by asking Him to get involved in every aspect of our lives. And just when life wore us down, God stepped in and sent us a sign of His existence that was beyond our scope of understanding. We had to put our previous beliefs about God aside because what was impossible to us was actually quite possible for God.

Miracle Child

My wife, Geralynn, and I had been married eight years and we were raising two awesome young boys when we decided to grow our family. We experienced a couple of miscarriages on our first attempts, and agreed it was important not to end on a negative note, so we turned to our doctor for answers. Testing revealed some small growths in my wife's uterus that were interfering with the supply of blood to the developing babies. Our obstetrician, Dr. Ling, assured us that this problem was treatable with only minor surgery. We were encouraged to hear the news, but more importantly, we now knew what to pray for. With the surgery scheduled we began to seek God for healing. We knew He heard our prayers when the Pastor interrupted service because he felt

God wanted him to pray for someone that needed healing for a problem in the abdomen. Geralynn knew it was for her and she went forward. She felt waves of heat rushing through her body as the pastor prayed for her. We did not realize what God had done until we went to surgery.

The morning of the surgery I sensed a strange stirring I had never felt before. Friends were praying for us, and I believed God just might show up. I tried to encourage Geralynn only minutes before the operation, but I could tell from her response that all my enthusiasm and constant jabbering was not having the impact I hoped for. She needed to relax and allow the medication to begin to do its work, so I kept this zeal to myself. The staff directed me to the waiting room as she disappeared down the hallway.

In the waiting room I settled down to read. Less than twenty minutes passed before a gray haired volunteer called my name. Doctor Ling wanted to speak with me in the hallway. I was confused by his presence because the surgery was scheduled to be over an hour in length. The doctor just stood there looking at his feet trying to tell me something. I do not remember what he said, but a thought rose up within me and

> This miracle opened our eyes to the power and kindness of God.

I blurted out, *"You can't find anything wrong. My wife is healed!"* With a puzzled look the Doctor replied, *"How did you know? You are correct. We could not find anything. Your wife is in the recovery room, and you can see her in a few minutes."* I tried to persuade him that God healed my wife, but

27

Doctor Ling looked even more confused. He was not sure what had happened; all he could say was that everything looked fine and Geralynn was in the recovery room. I could not believe what I was hearing. God had healed my wife, and the doctor was a witness.

Two weeks later we attended a follow up appointment. We thought Doctor Ling would look for other reasons behind the miscarriages because of the lack of physical evidence during surgery. His reply stunned us. *"I don't know what you believe, but all I know is that your wife is healed. The growths were there, I have the pictures. My diagnosis was not wrong, and all I can say is what she had is now gone. She is totally fine and able to have more children."* The doctor did not believe in miracles so he stuck to his facts and said goodbye to us.

A few months later Geralynn shared a dream with me. In the dream God showed her that she would have another child. Within a year God gave us our first daughter, Katelynn. To our surprise, God blessed us the following year with another daughter, Aubrey. Both girls were a direct result of that miracle and every time I look into their eyes, I see a loving Father who so graciously helped us. This miracle opened our eyes to the power and kindness of God. This event greatly impacted our lives and also profoundly affected our Doctor. Shortly after the birth of our second daughter, Doctor Ling excused himself from the delivery room. He was going to attend church with his son who had recently become a Christian. This was quite unusual since we knew he was a Buddhist. God used Geralynn's healing to plant a seed in that doctor's heart about His existence as well. Miracles have a way of impacting more people than we can ever imagine. Even my family was beginning to become more aware of God's continual presence.

Personal experiences have been a powerful tool in shaping my beliefs about God. Seeing God work in my family gave me something tangible to hold on to. It was now becoming clear why my mother and father had acted so strange when I was young. They were searching for proof of God's existence, and the miracle with my leg encouraged them to look deeper. Here I am, years later, having my own personal experiences with God, and now my children are trying to understand why I am acting so radically different. In the past it was quite easy to sway me on my theories and opinions about God, but now I am convinced of who He is for me. That is the life-changing power of a God experience.

We all need our own experience. The Bible is full of great stories about every-day people who witnessed the amazing power of God's handiwork. If He is as real as the Bible declares, then we all want to know that particular God. Not an imitation one, not an imaginary one, and not one trapped in the past. Each one of us wants a God who is willing to be everything He claims to be, today. You should refuse to sit in an old wooden pew, sing a couple of songs, toss some loose change in a basket once a week and be content that this is all God wants from you. You need a God who makes a difference in your life. You need an experience!

My opinions about God were being radically altered. Geralynn's healing was no coincidence. I decided to put more questions before God and see what would happen and it did not take long for Him to show up again.

God's Choice

Life was taking on new meaning. I greeted each day with an enthusiasm I had not felt in a long time. My excitement was contagious, and people were asking questions. I wanted a way to encourage others, but the words were difficult for me. I decided the right book might provide them with the freedom to open up to God at their own pace. With so many books to choose from, I knew I needed God's opinion on the matter. I placed my request before Him, and one book rose quickly to the top. *Prison to Praise,* by Merlin Carothers, it is an inspiring story of a soldier who experienced God in such a unique way that he became an Army Chaplin just so he could teach others about God. The following story is how God encouraged me to share this particular book with others.

When Sarah, an acquaintance, began to inquire about God I simply suggested that she read the book *Prison to Praise.* I thought the book may answer a few of her questions and give us something to talk about. It was a chance to get someone else's opinion on the book. Sarah read the book and recommended it to her sister and mother. All three devoured the book within a few short days. Sarah was so impressed that she mailed it to her boyfriend, Jack, in the Army. Within a month Sarah returned with the most amazing story.

Sarah discovered that Jack had undergone a spiritual transformation when she went to his graduation from basic training. The book's main character had captured Jack's attention. He enjoyed the stories that dealt with army life, but one particular story had a profound impact on him. Merlin Carothers was serving as a chaplain in Vietnam, when he began to witness some miraculous events while praying with the soldiers. Prayers were being answered in powerful ways both on the battlefield and at home, thousands of miles away. Jack was so stirred by the events he read that he shared his new book with the other recruits and it quickly made its way around the barracks. Soon, he and some other recruits decided to start their own prayer group. Their enthusiasm even prompted the Army Chaplin to join. In an attempt to draft others into their prayer group, the recruits passed the book onto the master drill sergeant.

Days later the sergeant returned with an amazing revelation. He confessed that he actually knew Merlin Carothers personally. The sergeant explained that he was one of the soldiers in Vietnam who were mentioned in the book. He actually attended those prayer meetings with Chaplin Carothers and personally witnessed some of the events. Since the soldiers are not named in the book the recruits pressed him on why he believed it referred to him.

The sergeant referred to a particular story involving a soldier who had a son with an unexplainable foot problem. The family tried doctors, braces, and special wraps, but nothing seemed to help the young boy. Pain made it impossible for him to walk or sleep without special assistance. The soldiers in Vietnam had agreed in prayer that God would intervene on the boy's behalf. A few weeks later this particular soldier received a letter from his wife stating that their son had stopped complaining about his feet. She noticed the change earlier, but she waited for a week before she felt confident enough to write. His wife mentioned the day that she noticed the transformation in their son's feet and attitude, and the soldier realized that his son was actually healed on the very same day they prayed for him. Every time Chaplin Carothers saw the soldier he would raise his arms and say, *"His feet still don't hurt yet."*

The master sergeant turned to the recruits and proclaimed that the boy in the story was actually his son. This was his personal God story! To verify his claim he produced a letter he saved from Vietnam which was the exact letter mentioned in the book. In it his wife describes how their son was healed. What an amazing story! Here stood a man who personally witnessed all they had just read. Not only had God placed this book into the hands of all these people, but it landed in the hands of a person who could totally confirm the truth of its contents.

As I started to ask questions, Sarah interrupted me to tell me that this was not the end of her story. *"There was more?"* I asked. *"Yes, and it only gets better!"* she replied. While Jack was sharing his story by the hotel pool, a stranger, only a few chairs away had been listening the entire time. The gentleman was so impacted by the events he had heard that he boldly interrupted to ask if he could read *Prison to Praise.* Sarah said she promptly handed him the book and then apologized for not being able to return the book. I assured her that if God wanted to keep it in circulation it was all right with me.

This particular story did not end there because Sarah returned a couple of days later to inform me that God was still at work with that one copy of *Prison to Praise.* Jack left a small marker in the book which contained his name, address and phone number. He forgot to remove it when Sarah had given it to the man by the pool. The gentleman decided to use that information to call Jack and thank him for the chance to read this extraordinary book. He went on to mention that he and his wife had recommitted their lives to following the Lord because of what they read.

> That day I decided that there are no coincidences in life.

During my drive home from work, I thanked the Lord for giving me such a wonderful story. It was amazing how God had orchestrated all these events. As I began to mull these things over, a quiet thought permeated my mind. *"You wanted to know which book."* That was right, I did ask for a confirmation and God actually answered my request. From that day forward I knew which book I would always recommend. In fact, I have handed out over two thousand copies of *Prison to Praise.* I have heard other great stories about that particular book, but none quite like Jack and Sarah's.

In the past I would have considered that series of events as purely random, and ignored them. But that day I decided there are no coincidences in life. There is no limitation to what God can do for us. We just have to keep our eyes open to new possibilities like I told my friend, Darren, in the next story.

Just Ask!

Darren and I have been great friends ever since high school. Every time I had the chance I would share my most recent God experience with him. Once, after hearing another account of what God was up to in my life, he made a very humorous comment: *"Dave, I think these God experiences are only for you. None of my other friends ever have stories like these."* I laughed because I knew that no one has exclusive rights to God. At times, God can seem quite elusive, but hiding from us is not part of His character. Actually, He is constantly searching for anyone who truly wants to hear from Him. I questioned Darren to see if he had ever asked God to give him an experience. I added, *"You have not, because you ask not."* He admitted he had never made such a simple request. He agreed that day to ask God to reveal Himself, and I prayed for God to act quickly. Twenty four hours later we were on the phone. This time Darren was telling me his own personal "God" experience, and it was nothing short of amazing.

This experience happened just as he was trying to start a new venture into Christian comedy.

Darren had been managing and scheduling shows all around the country, and on this particular day he had been on the phone all morning trying to arrange a deal with a businessman in another state to invest in his project. The investor was not showing any interest and simply told Darren he did not "*get*" the whole concept of Christian comedy. This put the project on hold.

In the meantime, one of the show's promotional video clips was on the internet making quite a hit. Being pretty humorous, the video clip was soon forwarded through numerous e-mail chains. That particular clip traveled worldwide, and even a soldier in Iraq requested more information. Darren was confident his idea would work; he was just having trouble locating the right investor.

Later that same day the investor's wife, by what seemed like "random" circumstances, received Darren's video clip through her e-mail. She enjoyed it so much that she forwarded it to her husband. As the investor watched the video he recognized the logo and knew if was from Darren's company. The investor phoned him and said, "*I get it, now!*" God had brought a simple e-mail to the desk of this man to help him understand Darren's objective. Darren was astonished at the way God arranged that experience for him. I told him, "*I guess it is not a 'me' thing anymore.*" He laughed, and now whenever we talk he has a new story for me.

> We just have to keep our eyes open to new possibilities.

If you ask each person you meet to tell you one of their personal God experiences, sadly, many will tell you, *"I don't have one."* If you are one of those people, then you need one. Are you ready to have your own unique God experience? It takes no effort. Ask and trust that God will show up. My only suggestion is twofold: do not tell God what to do, and do not expect God to answer with some huge display of power and light. God is not into theatrics and He likes to work through everyday life. However, if you are ready for an experience, it is time to ask for one of your own.

Here is how that request may sound:

"God, reveal yourself to me in some way so that I know you exist. Make it obvious to me and help me to see what you are doing. I ask this in Jesus' name."

God is actually easier to find than we think. When we are sincere and patient, He will answer. Signs of God's presence will appear in places you never imagined. I want you to know that God has not answered all my prayers in the ways I expected. He has, however, worked all things for good in my life (Roman 8:28). God answers all our requests in His own unique ways. After you receive an answer, make sure you ask again. The more you practice looking for God, the better you get to know Him.

> Truth without an experience is still just a theory.

An experience is what allows an idea to become a truth. Without a personal encounter a theory remains only a possibility. The Bible is full of truths, but without an experience they are simply theories. It is God's greatest joy for you to encounter and rely on His faithfulness. When we live out God's promises, our behavior will take on a confident expectation. Only that which we experience and trust will truly set us free.

To the Jews who had believed him, Jesus said, "If you hold to my teaching, you are really my disciples. Then you will know the truth, and the truth will set you free."
John 8:31-32 NIV

In closing, I would like you to rate your belief in the existence of God as my children did. I added a few more questions to help you think about on some other aspects of God. This is a good starting point, so take your time and be honest with yourself.

Fill in the blanks
(0 – 100%)

I believe in God _____%

I believe God hears me _____%

I believe God answers prayers _____%

I believe God wants to be my friend _____%

The most powerful way for God to reveal Himself to us is through a personal experience.

Helpful Biblical Principle

In that day you will no longer ask me anything. I tell you the truth, my Father will give you whatever you ask in my name. Until now you have not asked for anything in my name. Ask and you will receive, and your joy will be complete.

John 16:23-24 NIV

- *Chapter Three* -

Signs

"God's voice is found in the world around us."

Reckless Abandon

Telling someone God actually speaks is a tough statement to make. It can place you in a category you may not want to belong. At the risk of being labeled a fanatic, I would like to tell you God really speaks.

How I got to this point in my walk with God requires me to explain a few things. After abandoning the American dream and searching for God, I discovered something quite powerful in my investigation. The Bible tells us that Jesus promised to send His Spirit to live in anyone who believed in him. (John 14:15-17). This passage helped me understand that it was God's Spirit dwelling in me that opened my eyes to His work in my life. God was taking the time to help me understand who He was. My rapport with God was maturing, and I enjoyed the amount of involvement He had in my life. God, however, was not content with my level of understanding, and He decided that this needed to change.

In my studies I was drawn to the eleventh

chapter of Luke where it stated that we could ask for more of God's Holy Spirit. The word *"more"* impressed upon my mind as I meditated on this verse. Finally, I asked myself, *"If all these amazing things I experienced so far were by His Spirit, then what would happen if I had more?"* I was excited about this God stuff, so I decided to seek out everything there was. I abandoned all I knew and jumped in with this simple prayer:

"Father, I ask for more of your Holy Spirit to fill me and guide me. Immerse me into your powerful Spirit and reveal all there is to know about you. I ask this in the name of Jesus Christ, your son."

Then, God spoke!

Prison Bound

I was enjoying the drive. The sun was out and the radio was playing one of those catchy songs. Before I realized it, what seemed like a "random" thought took me by surprise. *"Go to the prisons and preach the gospel."* This was not a thought I had ever entertained before. I mulled the idea over in my mind for a few seconds. No one I knew was practicing this kind of Christianity. Preaching in prison was a radical concept, and it was definitely too progressive for me. My sharp mind saw through this foolish thought, and I responded with a prompt, *"No way!"* My inexperience with God made me believe He would never lead me that far outside my comfort zone.

I dismissed the prison idea, but God persisted.

As the days passed, the idea occasionally floated through my mind as a constant gentle reminder, but my determination to avoid the idea never let those thoughts stay very long. God knew I was not going to move forward on this idea, so He decided to encourage me again.

Days later, during another drive, I made an abrupt stop at an intersection, and everything not tied down shot forward. One of the books that were crammed under the seat slid into full view and immediately caught my attention. It was appropriately titled *Prison to Praise*, and the word *"prison"* caught my eye. Immediately, I was pondering the prospect of preaching in the prisons once again. As one scenario after another raced through my mind, I realized that these unusual circumstances may be connected. Based upon what I had learned from earlier my experiences with God, I felt He was using the word *prison* to get my attention.

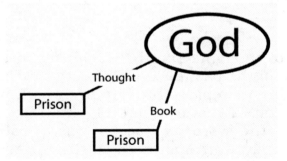

I usually like to write off these situations as mere *"coincidence"*, but I knew God was somehow involved. The more I thought about it, the more I realized I had no desire to spend time with those who are incarcerated, so the idea was cast aside and forgotten once again.

But God did not give up so easily, and the signs just kept coming. While immersed in the Bible, a particular story jumped off the page. Jesus used the story of a King to explain to his disciples how God was going to separate His chosen people from the ungodly ones. The King (God) reveals that the person who meets the needs of the thirsty, the hungry, or the naked would in essence be helping the King. This I understood, because when we lend a hand to the people around us we are actually helping God himself. It was Jesus' last example that sent my mind reeling because he stated that those who visited the sick or anyone in prison would actually be visiting the King (Matthew 25). It was right in line with what I felt God was asking me to do, and this verse specifically mentioned visiting others in prison.

> Every time I thought God spoke to me, a battle with doubt and uncertainty ensued.

A flurry of thoughts raced through my head at 200 mph. All of the past encounters with this prison concept began to replay through my mind. What was going on? Everywhere I went I kept encountering the word "*prison.*" I was perplexed. Could God really want me to go to the prisons? I began to see a pattern emerging, and I did not like the outcome.

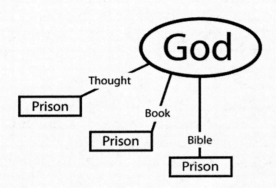

A battle with doubt and uncertainty ensued. I began to question my line of thinking. Could God really be asking me to do something this irrational and illogical? Was my mind coming up with another scheme to make life more interesting? If this was the Lord, where would I go from here?

I decided to seek God's advice on the subject. He had answered me before—maybe He would again. If this request was actually from God, I needed a response that would stifle my doubt! Attending Sunday church was fine, but visiting prisoners was a whole new level for me. The prayer was simple and to the point. I told God that if He wanted me to go into the prisons, He would need to confirm this message. I needed a little more assurance; otherwise, my wife's case for my insanity would only get better.

When three events share a common theme I now step back in prayer to let God know He has my attention. Playing dumb with God has never worked. He knows all my tricks, especially when I am trying to avoid something. Asking for a confirmation is an excellent way for me to clarify what is from God and what is not. God has no problem when we ask for confirmations because it makes us focus on Him even more.

This idea, of God confirming His message, is revealed in the Bible through the story of Gideon and the fleece (Judges 6). God was asking Gideon to rise up and fight a great Midianite army on behalf of Israel. Being neither a warrior nor a great man of stature, Gideon lacked the faith in himself and in God to bring about such a victory. Gideon, however, was willing to go if he could be certain that what he was hearing was truly from God, so he asked for a sign. God answered his request by keeping a fleece of wool dry overnight while the grass in the morning was soaked with dew, then God made the fleece wet and kept all the ground dry the following night.

What I like about the story is that God sent more signs to inspire Gideon even though he did not request them. To ensure God got all the credit for the victory He trimmed his troops down to just 300 men a few days before the battle. Gideon's needed a new level of courage if he was going to face 150,000 Midianites with only a handful of men, and God knew what it would take to strengthen his faith. He instructed Gideon to sneak into the enemy's camp and listen for a sign. While hiding among the enemy, he overhears a soldier telling his comrades his most recent dream. Upon conclusion of the vision another Midianite soldier suggests that this dream could only mean that Gideon's army would destroy them. Gideon knew only God could have made these men say such things, and he returned to his troops so full of faith that he led his army to one of the greatest victories in Israel's history (Judges 7).

God is eager to confirm anything He says to us because He wants each of us to be men and women of great faith. I was new to hearing God's leadings and a boost in faith was definitely in order. I asked God for another *'prison'* sign, but honestly I did not fully expect a reply. What happened next took me by surprise. A few of us visited a local church to listen to a guest speaker. Upon entering the building I noticed a banner hanging in the foyer that read, *"Join our prison ministry. Sign up below."* How was this possible? Right before my eyes was my destiny written on a church sign. All I could do was whimper the words, *"Oh no!"* Someone asked what was wrong, but I knew they would not understand, so I sent them on ahead. I lingered by the table trying to decide what to do. Unsure, I took a form, shoved it into my pocket and joined my friends. I knew the banner was no random accident! God was speaking very clearly!

> God wants each one of us to become men and women of great faith.

That night I sought God in prayer. With doubt removed, it was now only a question of when and where. God needed to know how I truly felt about His prison idea. I discussed my limited knowledge of the Bible, my lack of motivation, my busy schedule, my dislike for the type of element found in prisons, and my lack of nerve. I shared everything in my heart: the good, the bad and the ugly. Going to a prison in my spare time was not a dream of mine, but throughout this process I could tell I was beginning to accept the idea. I was ready to move forward so I specifically asked God to open a door to help me locate someone with the knowledge of how to set up a prison bible study. If necessary, I would return to the church that had the prison ministry, but I wanted God to reveal his path one more time. I could see the events unfolding.

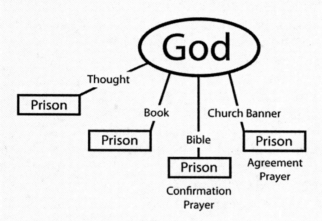

I knew God had heard me because I felt a peace about the entire matter. Time marched on into the Fall, and the routine of work allowed me to push the prisons to the back of my mind. It had been a month since I told God my whole heart, and without an answer I felt He had found someone better suited for the task. Actually, this was not the case. He was just saving His best sign for last. One I would never forget.

One day someone informed me that a part-time worker at the other end of the building had heard of my belief in God and wished to speak with me. Joe was a temporary worker who filled in when an employee was absent. While covering my position early that year he noticed the Christian literature in my office which gave him an impression of my faith. During lunch I stopped by and introduced myself. Through the course of our discussion we learned that we shared a similar passion for God. After chatting for a short time he cut to the chase and stated, *"I really asked you down here to see if you have ever thought about going into the prisons to teach the Bible. As a Chaplin I run a local prison ministry and we can always use more help."* I was speechless. The Lord actually sent a Prison Chaplin to my job as an answer to prayer. What else could I do but say, *"Where do I go and when should I be there?"* WOW! I asked for a sign, and God sent one. I asked for a person and He sent a one. Every direction I turned, the Lord was right there with an answer. I did not completely understand why God wanted me in that prison, but once inside I watched Him touch many lives. Working with the prisoners also taught me a lot about God's love. I may not have been the most willing participant at first, but God worked it out for everyone's good.

God continues to use signs like these to direct my life. I never know how or when He is going to send me one, but I have become confident of this: there are no coincidences!

Once God begins to reach out to you, you will find He likes to use signs that come from the most random places. Remember, if you think it might be God, just ask! You have nothing to lose and everything to gain. With this new understanding you will begin to see and hear God in a whole new way. One young man once told me, *"Hearing God's voice was easier than I had ever imagined. Once you tune into His voice you cannot turn it off."*

> If you think it might be God just ask!

Do not be surprised if one quiet little thought sends your life in a whole new direction. Keep reading and you will find out what I mean.

Anything but That, God!

The church we attended moved into a new building, and things were settling down when our pastor's father became ill. He made the decision to step down from his position because he was not sure how long he would be gone. We were all sad to see him go. The Bishop arranged for other ministers to fill in while we prayed for God to send us a new leader.

During my prayer times I felt I heard God say that I should step in as the pastor. God's request seemed strange because I had no experience or training in church ministry. I was acting as the youth leader, but our family had only been attending this church for a little over a year, so I shrugged off the idea. However, I was pressed by the thought enough times that I was willing to tell my wife, just to get her opinion. Geralynn was not sure about the idea and felt it was impracticable given our family situation. Again, I was willing to give up the notion quickly because it seemed quite illogical given my circumstances.

This only prompted God to step in and turn up the heat. A few days later I found myself helping a young lady with a problem at work. Jennifer was so taken by my patience and encouragement that she commented, "*You would make a great pastor.*" I was shaken by her comment and kept the matter to myself. Soon, God put the word "*pastor*" around me a couple more times and I saw the beginnings of another theme. Now I was more confident that being pastor was God's idea, so I approached my wife a second time. She assured me I was mistaken and explained how the church was too small to provide a sufficient salary to replace my current income. We knew with four children that our time was also too limited to take on such a big commitment. In rational terms my wife was right. However, we soon discovered that God was working outside our realm of logic again.

The Bible teaches that sometimes God makes requests that may be contrary to how we currently operate, as Joshua learned when he attacked Jericho (Joshua 6). Joshua's army achieved many victories under God's leadership, but when it came to Jericho God changed all the rules. This time God asked Israel to simply march around the walls of the city, blow their trumpets and return to their tents. For seven days Joshua and his army obeyed God's word, even when they felt they were strong enough to overtake the city by force. On the seventh day just after the last horn blew the walls fell down without warning, and the battle was won in moments.

I was feeling like Joshua. There was just no good explanation for why God wanted me to be a pastor, but the signs kept coming. This situation required another confirmation from God. I wanted a sign that even a blind man could not miss. Pursuing this idea would have major implications, and our family could not afford for me to take this lightly. I decided I would take the position if that was God's true desire for my life, but *I just needed a really good sign!* With that decision in mind I sat down with my journal to put my heart before the Lord. I wrote down all my doubts and concerns, with nothing left unsaid.

After placing the final words on the page I sat back to let it all sink in. No more than five minutes passed before the telephone rang. This was no ordinary phone call. It was Dad, who broke four of his cardinal rules in life to make this particular call. He made the call himself, and I knew dialing the phone was our stepmother's task since his favorite arm had been immobilized. Dad's favorite time to call was late in the evening to avoid any unnecessary charges, and here it was only ten in the morning. The grandchildren, when over, always had top priority of his attention and I could hear them playing in the background. Finally, dad usually only called if he had a question and kept our conversation to less than five minutes, but today he just wanted to talk.

I inquired about the purpose of the call, and Dad said he felt God had given him a message for me. I was on the edge of my seat as he read me a little scripture tucked away in the book of John.

To this John replied, "A man can receive only what is given him from heaven.
John 3:27 NIV

The verse did not seem like any great words of wisdom, so I asked Dad what they meant to him. His reply sealed my fate. *"As I read this, I felt like God was telling me He wants to give you something. You are not to worry about how you will do it. God just wants you to agree and He will take care of everything else."* Dad asked whether it made sense to me. Knowing what I wrote in my journal minutes earlier, I let him know that his message was just what I needed to hear. Before dad passed away a few years later I did have the opportunity to tell him exactly what that conversation had done for me.

I told Geralynn the whole story about what happened with Dad. She knew my father, and she was convinced that only God could have gotten him to break his predictable patterns. We agreed it was time to bring the matter to the Bishop, and for a moment I thought I had discovered a loophole. Part of my human nature was still looking for a way out. I knew I could not be pastor without the Bishop's consent, and I felt that with no formal training it would be out of the question. The Bishop was bound to see this as a poor option for our church. Financially, I was tied to my career and unable to leave for any ministry training. This brought a sigh of relief to Geralynn and me. We actually thought we had discovered the one locked door that had no key.

We scheduled a dinner with the Bishop during his next visit to the area. The food seemed to lack any flavor, and just before dessert I mentioned that God was leading me to step in as pastor of the church. The words seemed to fall flat on the table, and I half expected some laughter to erupt. The laughter never came and the Bishop quietly wiped his mouth and said, *"When I first met you God told me that you would lead one of my churches. I was waiting for you to hear it from God yourself. Now that we are all in agreement we can ordain you in a few weeks and install you as pastor as quickly as the first Sunday of the next month."* I was astounded and asked about the need for training. He replied, *"If God wants you to be head of this church, who am I to stand in His way?"*

God met my wife and I at every roadblock, opening doors we never imagined. My father attended the ordination service, and he was able to hear me preach several times; for that I have been eternally thankful.

As you can see, God carefully placed all these signs around us so that we would not miss the path He had chosen for us. As you look for direction in your life, God will open your eyes to His leadings. The more you look for God, the more you will become conscious that He is always beside you. I had to learn how God communicates, and so do you. Perhaps God has been speaking to you, but you may have been totally unaware. The moment we are willing to extend the smallest trust in God's existence we become spiritually altered to hear His voice. This truth is foundational to believing in God (John 10:3-5, 27). So take a few moments to step out from your existing mind set and ask God to speak to you. Here is a prayer designed to help you recognize God's response.

> The more you look for God, the more you will become conscious that He is always beside you.

"Father, speak to me in a way that I can understand your voice. Give me the eyes to see and the ears to hear what you are saying. I ask for your guidance in Jesus' name."

Maybe it is time you pray for the baptism of the Holy Spirit. Turn back to page 40 and ask God for this special gift. It just might be the boost you need to propel you into a closer relationship with Him.

Try not to ignore God by convincing yourself that what you hear is simply *"a coincidence."* Seeing God in this busy world is truly a special gift.

> *Ears to hear and eyes to see — both are gifts from the LORD.*
> Proverbs 20:12 NLT

Be alert! The God I know speaks!

Task at Hand

Ask God to speak to you. Then look for signs of His voice and write down what you hear.

I believe God is asking me to...

_____

_____

_____

_____

_____

_____

_____

Signs God sent me to confirm His word:

_____

_____

_____

_____

_____

_____

_____

God's words may be found

in a friend's voice,

the next show you watch,

on the pages of your

favorite magazine,

in tonight's dream, or

any other device

He chooses.

Remember...

God has the whole universe at His disposal. Sending us a message is not a problem!

Helpful Biblical Principle

Jesus answered, "It is written: 'Man does not live on bread alone, but on every word that comes from the mouth of God."

Matthew 4:4 NIV

Chapter Four

Surprised by God

"God wants to talks to us."

Every person has some idea of who God is for them. Sadly, many people's version of God cannot accomplish much of anything. Too many Gods today are based mostly on theory and conjecture with very little experience. That is what can happen if you believe in God with your head and not with your heart. God is tired of being left at church on Sunday, because He understands the value of His friendship. The God I know is searching for people who are willing to venture outside of their current perceptions and honestly seek Him out.

God is convinced that an alliance with Him is our greatest reward. The Bible tells us that God's word is powerful, living and active (Hebrews 4:12), we cannot hear His voice and remain unchanged. His words create something inside of us that turns fears into strengths and weaknesses into assets. The possibilities of what we can achieve in this life become limitless the moment we recognize and obey the voice of God.

> God creates something inside you that turns fears into strengths and weaknesses into assets.

The Bible is filled with stories about God working in the lives of ordinary men and women. As each person discovered something about God's true nature and then aligned themselves to flow with Him, their lives took on greater significance. They stepped out from the norm of their day and left behind legacies for all of us to follow. God is still revealing himself today, but some of us are still not aware of His presence. This is because it has become difficult to sense God with our world so out of balance. But there is good news, all it takes to realign yourself is to take one small step towards God and He will take one step towards you. God loves an honest seeker and does not scoff at being investigated. This is where you get to decide. Are you happy with what God has done with you so far, or do you want more? My decision to step out has not always been easy, but experiences have taught me that God truly is my best friend.

God Will Speak to Anyone!

Tucked away in the twentieth chapter of Genesis is an interesting story about a man named Abraham. Abraham trusted God so much that the Bible says they became friends (*James 2:23*). God spoke to Abraham and called him from his homeland with the promise that He would give him new lands, a place that would belong to his children for generations to come. While en route, Abraham was summoned to appear in the courts of kings as he crossed their territories. Abraham knew that the kings of his time liked to take on many wives, and this made Abraham decide to introduce his wife, Sarah, as his sister. He did this out of fear of being killed because Sarah was very beautiful.

Believing Sarah was Abraham's sister, the King of Gerar, Abimelech, brought her to his palace hoping to make her his wife. Abimelech never got the chance to be intimate with Sarah because God stepped in and revealed her true identity. In a dream God made it known to the king that Sarah was in fact Abraham's wife and if he continued with the marriage it would have a devastating effect on his kingdom. God instructed Abimelech to return Sarah and have Abraham pray a blessing over his family to lift a curse. The king confronted Abraham and discovered that Sarah was indeed his wife. Abimelech gave Abraham land, servants, livestock, and silver to compensate for any shame he may have caused. Then Abraham prayed for the king and left.

Even though the king had no knowledge at of Abraham's God, he still heard Him vividly in a dream. Trusting wholeheartedly that he had heard from God, the king obeyed by returning Sarah. Abimelech went out of his way to honor Abraham with expensive gifts, land, animals and servants just to make sure all was forgiven, even when Abraham initially caused the problem by lying. Abimelech must have been quite shaken by the dream because God never mentioned any gifts. Well, if an unbelieving, heathen king can hear God that clearly, so can you and I.

The Bible also reveals that God spoke to all kinds of people, not just the ones He considered his friends. To my surprise, God had discussions with murderers, complainers, liars, and schemers of all types. He even spoke with Satan. Popular teachings had led me to believe that God was angry with me for all the things I had done. This made it difficult for me to look to God for help, but my new experiences were revealing someone completely different. A person who is merciful, kindhearted, and caring; who chooses to forget whatever we ask Him to forgive (Isaiah 43:25). God chooses this because if He were to make our faults and wanderings a priority then He would have to turn His back on Jesus' sacrifice to reconcile us. God does not speak to us just because of our sin; He reaches out to us because He is focused on the life we would miss out on if we continue in the wrong direction. God always chooses to restore His relationships with us rather than destroy them with anger and judgment (Isaiah 1:18).

> God is not focused on sin because He is too consumed with life.

Amazingly, God does speak to everyone and His words are always full of encouragement. For some it may be to move them into a place of blessing and growth as it was for Abraham. For others it may be words of caution intended to prevent problems or avert a disaster as it was for King Abimelech. It is always up to us to decide if we will listen and respond. However God decides to speak to us, His voice is exactly what we need, when we need it. God is so in tune with His people that He can speak to every one of us according to our unique qualities, as some of my friends found out.

The Deer Hunter

Jim was going through a stressful time in his life. Using the chance to encourage him, I expounded on how God is willing to converse with us and assist us in our everyday life. I related a couple of my stories and then expressed that he needed his own experience with God to be filled with faith. Jim decided it was time to ask God to reveal himself. I saw him again that following Monday, and this was the story he shared with me.

It was the night before opening day of deer season, and Jim was an avid hunter. During the night he had a powerful dream. He awoke sweating, breathing hard, and feeling like it had actually happened. In the dream Jim remembered shooting a buck in a foggy section of woods on his neighbor's property. Every detail was clearly etched upon his mind. He could picture everything—the trees, the fog, the buck, and even the shot. Upon waking, Jim concluded he needed to hunt the section of land he recognized from his dream. His father tried to dissuade him because they had never been successful hunting deer on that particular piece of land. Jim was determined, so he ended up hunting alone. He ventured into the woods and located the perfect spot while it was still dark. As the sun rose, a fog rolled in off the corn, and in that moment he realized this was the exact place from his dream. Upon further inspection, he noticed that even the layout of the trees and brush were identical.

Jim became nervous because if this was going to turn out like his dream, the buck would be just over his shoulder. With his heart racing he turned to look and there stood the buck. After calming himself, he set his sights and fired. The deer crashed to the ground just as it did in his dream.

The similarities between the events of the day and what happened the night before were so exact that Jim sat there for twenty minutes just getting the courage up to stand and claim his kill.

Jim dragged the deer to his truck and while taking care of the details a doe appeared in the corn a few rows down from where he was parked. He was not sure if he wanted to fill all his tags in one day, but since it looked like an easy shot he decided to take it. Down went another deer with only one shot. After racking another shell he walked down to tag the doe, but when he approached the spot where the deer fell, he could not find it anywhere. There was no trace of blood or tracks of any kind. He continued on down a few more rows looking for signs of the doe, but the only tracks he noticed were his own. He searched the corn thoroughly, because he did not want to leave a wounded deer.

After a while he returned to his truck thinking he only imagined the deer, but there next to the truck he found the spent shotgun shell, so he knew he had taken a shot. Things did not seem right, so once he got home he took his gun out for a couple of test shots, and each was significantly off by about ten feet. After examining his gun he noticed the new barrel was not fully seated, which caused it to shoot inaccurately. With the barrel so misaligned Jim realized it would have been impossible for him to shoot even the buck at that range. Based on the way the gun was shooting he should have completely missed. A little thought made him realize that only God could have directed the bullet and given him the kill. There was no other way. Jim knew his gun, and he knew his shooting skills, so there was no way he could have brought down the buck.

He looked straight at me and said, *"God is real, because that is the only way I could have shot the buck!"* I knew Jim needed the encouragement and God revealed Himself in a way that made the most sense to him. That is how God works. God spoke to this avid hunter as a hunter.

Have you ever been drawn to read a book and found an answer to one of life's problems? That was God. Ever notice how your friends call at the right time with the perfect words just when your life looks so hopeless and you are about to quit. That was God. He has always been there, and He is trying to get your attention. The idea of events being a coincidence is just not logical! If you want God to speak to you, you need only a hungry heart. There is no other requirement, as Kevin discovered.

Zero to Sixty

Kevin and I got along quite well, and he often asked me about my God experiences. Most of the time he tried to logically explain what he believed may have happened as he considered every possible angle to my stories. Most discussions just led to more questions. Kevin reached the point where he wanted to know the truth about God for himself, so I suggested, *"Why not just ask God to show himself to you in some way. Let God be God and just be open to whatever happens."* He agreed and off he went.

One evening Kevin finally gathered enough

courage to ask God to reveal Himself in a way that would let him know He is real. The words Kevin used did not matter, because it simply came down to his open heart. That small request allowed God to turn his world upside down. In a few short days Kevin returned with a strange expression on his face that looked like Mr. Rational had encountered the unexplainable. This is his story.

During the fall Kevin's friend Mike was hurt while they were playing soccer. The injury required the leg to be iced. After the drive home Kevin reminded Mike not to forget to take his bag of ice, which was now mostly water, with him. The next day as Kevin went about his usual routine, he noticed Mike's bag of ice still on the floor of the car. Upon inspection he found the bag full of ice cubes just as it was from the match. The temperatures that week were above freezing during the day and just below at night. Kevin knew that if it was below freezing the bag would have been just one big block of ice and if it was warm it would have been completely melted. Logically, a day later the ice would never still be in the individual cube form. Besides what he had seen yesterday was half melted. What he saw was scientifically impossible.

Kevin searched for a logical answer, but found none. Later that day Kevin gave me the whole account of what happened. I was not able to explain the ice, and you could tell by Kevin's reaction he was perplexed. He asked me if I believed God had formed the cubes, but I could not answer that question. It was Kevin's experience, and that was for to him to determine.

Kevin contemplated that ice for a few days. Finally, he approached me and mentioned that he felt like he had gone from zero to sixty with God. He said, *"Just a couple of days ago I was as far from believing in God as anyone could be and yet overnight I actually believe."* I explained that an experience changes everything. Once you encounter God you cannot walk away unchanged. The thought of what God did will stay in your heart forever.

Kevin asked if there was more he should know about God, and at that moment I explained the miracle of complete forgiveness in Jesus Christ. God is always offering you this free gift, but you must be willing to accept it. *"When you are ready, the prayer is quite simple."* (Page 20) I left him alone to think it through.

A few days later Kevin found me working in my office. He told me he surrendered his life to God and accepted His forgiveness in Jesus' sacrifice. I asked him, *"Have you noticed that the grass looks greener, the sky looks bluer, and the reds were redder?"* With wide eyes he replied, *"This is bizarre. That was exactly what I was thinking! I was just looking out my window and thought that the grass looked so green, the sky looked super blue and this one red car looked extra red."* I laughed and told him, *"From now on you will see life in a whole new way"*. That day he got his new spiritual DNA.

> The most amazing thing about the voice of God is that it is exactly what you need when you need it.

Kevin still thinks about what happened and

comments about wanting to hear more from God. That experience was exactly what Kevin needed, and it made it easier for him to trust in God. He is beginning to understand how God speaks and that is all he needs to follow Him.

Today is the Day

God is so creative that He speaks to each of us in a way that is as unique as we are. I am always surprised at the ways God has spoken to me in the past. At times even my wife has had to sit up and take notice. We had not been believers very long before God began asking us to get baptized. I discussed it with my wife, and she felt we were all right since we had been baptized at birth. The Lord tugged at my heart and brought the idea of baptism around to me in so many ways I knew I had to go through with it. A few months after my baptism, my wife began to get the inclination that God wanted her to get baptized. She struggled with the idea, but as time progressed she knew it was the Lord's desire.

Geralynn is good at hearing from God, but as it is with all of us it is sometimes hard to get the courage up to go forward. I asked her a number of times if we should see the pastor about getting baptized, but she did not want to do it at church. We finally came up with the idea of baptizing her at our cottage on a lake up north. Once summer rolled around I asked her every chance I could to see which day was a good day to get baptized. Either she was too busy or the water was too cold, so I waited patiently until she was ready.

I like to get up early in the morning to read and pray, since quiet moments are hard to find at our cottage, especially with four children. As I meditated on the words I had been reading, a loud thought kept cutting in. *"Today's the day!"* Then again, *"Today's the day!"* Over and over it played. I asked God to bring some clarity to the situation, and at that moment I knew what the words meant. God was showing me that today was the day Geralynn was going to be baptized. I realized it needed to be done, but I did not want to force the subject. That was God's job, but at least I could ask. In fact the moment my wife peeked her head out of the bedroom I quickly shot out the words, *"Good morning, Today's the day!"* She looked perplexed when she asked me what I meant by that comment. I proudly replied, *"Today, I am going to baptize you."* I expected her to sidestep the issue and move on to more important details of the day like breakfast, but she simply replied, *"Sounds good."* That day we baptized her and everything went fine. No fireworks, but we felt we had accomplished what God had told us to do.

The best part of this story happened a few months later. We were back at home when I over-heard my wife talking in another room about my ability to hear God's voice. The conversation sounded interesting, so I decided to listen in. Geralynn explained how she had just woken up at the cottage last summer and heard someone say *"Today's the day!"* The voice was very distinct, but no one was in the room. She heard it again, and knew it was God telling her she needed to be baptized that day. What really surprised her was when I mentioned the exact words she heard the minute she emerged from the bedroom.

I rounded the corner and asked why she did not tell me about this confirmation last summer. She just smiled and confessed that she was caught off guard and just forgot. That gentle voice along with my response was her sign to step out and obey.

God has a tendency of making requests that sometimes seem to defy any rational explanation. Moving forward when God calls requires a new fortitude, since we all operate from a set of rules that makes us feel safe, known as our worldly knowledge. The good news is that when God speaks to us in these personal ways, it creates the strength and courage we need to step out of our comfort zone and act on His word. His goal is to teach us how to rely more on Him and less on ourselves. Trusting in God requires us to take many small steps of faith. Each experience helps us understand that He is for us and not against us (Romans 8:31). To move forward means we have to leave something behind. Maybe now is your time.

> God's goal is to teach us to rely more on Him and less on ourselves.

Jim experienced God in the woods, Kevin discovered Him through a bag of ice, and Geralynn heard Him in the quiet of morning. Each one of them was willing to let God do something new. Have you given God the chance to prove Himself on your behalf? Release God from any constraints you may have placed on Him so that you can experience His full power working in your life. When times get tough, and they will, what kind of God do you want on your side?

Let us close with a powerful little prayer:

"Lord, I do not know you as well as I should. I ask that you reveal your love and commitment to me in a powerful way. Open up my heart to receive the faith that you exist and the courage to follow your call. In Jesus' name. Amen."

Task at Hand

We know God wants to get involved so let us give one problem over to Him and see what He can do. Expect God to show up and turn your problems into victories, your anxieties into peace, and your confusion into wisdom.

God, I need your help with...

_____

_____

_____

_____

- CONFIRMATIONS -

_____

_____

_____

_____

_____

We are one small step away from greatness and one fear away from ordinary.

Helpful Biblical Principle

For I know the plans I have for you," declares the LORD, "plans to prosper you and not to harm you, plans to give you hope and a future. Then you will call upon me and come and pray to me, and I will listen to you. You will seek me and find me when you seek me with all your heart. I will be found by you," declares the LORD...

Jeremiah 29:11-14 NIV

Chapter Five

No Coincidences

"Life is a series of interwoven events."

In life there are no random twists of fate, no meaningless coincidences. Everything in this life has a purpose. Once you understand the power of God's goodness, you begin to recognize the detail He has put into designing your life. Each event has been carefully chosen just for you. So neither you nor your life is an accident.

As our hearts and minds begin to open up to the possibility that God may be more than we ever imagined, we need to address an item of some significance—the term *coincidence*. When this word is applied to any two situations, the subtly of God's involvement can be quickly swept under the rug and forgotten. A closer investigation reveals why the word *coincidence* should never be used. Webster defines it as, *"an event or circumstance relating in someway to other events by chance, not by design."* God does nothing by chance (Romans 8:28). Our goal is to begin to view life from the perspective that **all events are jointly and mutually put together for a purpose** so God can work something new in your life.

There are no good or bad circumstances with God; just a means to an end. As you move beyond the idea of calling a series of unexplainable events a coincidence, or accidental, you will begin to see life in a whole new dimension. Take the time to put aside your cynical views and take a good look into God's true nature, allow God the freedom to reveal Himself in your life. The following stories illustrate how creative God can be as He orchestrates situations in my life and others around me.

An Answer to Prayer

There is nothing more frustrating than the clicking sound of a car that will not start. After a couple of attempts I realized the battery was dead. My initial response was to grumble and complain about why these things happen at such inconvenient times. It had been a long day, and I wanted to relax, so changing the battery was the last thing on my mind. After sizing up the situation I came to the conclusion that I could remove the battery and reach the store before closing time. As I began to extract the battery, multiple obstacles robbed me of precious time. The battery was buried under a layer of brackets and bolts. My frustration grew as closing time approached. I successfully freed the battery with just enough time to complete my objective.

> God puts great detail into designing your life.

While working under the hood I remembered that my friend, Steve, was employed at this particular store. Our last conversation rolled through my mind and I was beginning to feel as if God wanted our paths to cross. While preparing for the trip to the store I grew more confident that this was no longer a battery problem; it was a God event in the works. Thoughts about Steve raced through my head, so I knew I needed to pray for the situation. I decided God allowed my battery to fail at the perfect time so I would have to meet up with Steve. I had not seen him in several weeks, and I was not quite sure of what God had in mind.

During the drive to the store my frustration gave way to peace. I sought God for advice on the matter. Why Steve? What was the matter? I arrived shortly before closing time, and a voice on the public address system announced that the store would close in ten minutes. I located a battery and then began to scour the aisles until the last possible second hoping to catch a glimpse of Steve. Nothing. I even questioned the cashier about his whereabouts as I checked out, but she did not even know who Steve was. The store closed and I was forced to leave. In route to my car I told God, *"I know you sent me here to see Steve. Since I do not see him, I will just pray for him."* I was confident that this was God's leading! With each step I asked for God's protecting power to cover Steve. Then just as I was loading the battery into my car a quiet voice asked. *"Is that you, Mr. Jackson?"* It was Steve.

In my excitement I told Steve how God had used a dead battery to arrange our meeting. For Steve it was a direct answer to prayer. Earlier that day Steve was struggling, and he knew if he could talk to me it would raise his spirits. Without my address or telephone number, he made a simple prayer for our paths to cross. Steve's prayer put me in the parking lot at the exact time he reported to work as a night stocker. If I had removed the battery any sooner or left the store any earlier, we would have completely missed each other. Steve was greatly encouraged, and I told him everything that God put on my heart, and then we prayed. Both Steve and I were moved knowing that our meeting was totally orchestrated by God. What else could I expect?

Life changed, and now run-of-the-mill, everyday events were becoming extraordinary. Trips to the store, friendly conversations, a wrong turn, or any unplanned visitors were just a small step away from being a God adventure. Nothing was too small or insignificant. God was turning out to be master of the random as my friend Bill found out.

Obvious

Bill was job shadowing and observing the everyday duties of my job when a comment about fasting was brought up. I remarked on the matter and quickly refocused our group to the task at hand. I forgot about the conversation, but after work Bill approached me and asked me about fasting. I explained there were times in my life when I was willing to sacrifice some creature comfort, such as food, as I prayed for direction in my life. We discussed the matter further and then headed home.

The next day a different group gathered in my area at lunch to discuss the Bible. Someone suggested we all fast and ask God for His direction on how we could impact our building for God in the upcoming year. Bill and I glanced at each other and smiled. I was sure God was giving me a message because this was the second time I heard about fasting in the last two days. Later that afternoon I spoke with Bill about hearing from God. We discussed how God can speak to us in themes. I showed him my diagram and I shared a couple of my God experiences with him. Bill left encouraged, and I went home to see what God was up to.

That night I prayed to see what God wanted from me. As I read through some verses in the Bible I began to understand that this message was actually for Bill and not me. This made me a little uneasy. How do you tell someone God is sending them a message? I was just not sure how to bring this matter to Bill's attention. I decided that this situation would be a great way to test my thoughts and see if they were really from God. Bill's reaction would be my confirmation.

The next day I shared with Bill some biblical reasons for fasting, and then inquired about how he felt about fasting. He mentioned that the idea of it bothered him all night. I stepped out of my comfort zone and informed him of what God had told me the night before. Bill felt the same way, so I encouraged him to look for more signs to prove this was actually from God. I explained that if God was leading him to fast, somebody could walk through my door and say, "*I want to know more about this fasting thing.* It was important that Bill got his own confirmation from God.

Amazingly, one hour later, a young man walked in my door and said, "*I want to know more about this fasting thing.*" Bill looked startled because it was the exact words I had used earlier. Bill's face turned a nice shade of red, and I just had to laugh. God met us in a truly amazing way. Bill followed through on the fast because he knew it was God's desire. That small encounter with God's voice greatly increased our levels of faith.

God needs nothing from you except a desire to listen and a willingness to take action

As we search for God we must be careful that our worldly logic and reasoning does not hinder us from trusting His voice. If our goal is to increase our ability to sense God's presence then we must consider the condition of our heart. We do this by asking ourselves some tough questions:

- *Am I willing to commit myself to do whatever God asks of me no matter how illogical it seems or how uncomfortable it makes me feel?*

- *Do I harbor any unbelief toward God that would limit Him from working in my life?*

There is nothing God needs from you except a desire to hear Him and the willingness to take action as I found out.

A Time to Write

I awoke one morning with this nagging thought that I should write a book about my experiences with God. The thought became so loud and repetitive that by breakfast I confided in my wife, "*I think God wants me to write a book.*" Geralynn, lovingly replied, "You *can't write. Your English is terrible."* We laughed, because she was right. Chemistry and Physics are easier concepts for me than sentence structure, vocabulary, and proper punctuation. I became convinced that writing a book was just a wild passing thought. My old friend, rationality, came to my rescue again and set me free from a potentially difficult situation.

That day some friends stopped by at lunch, and we discussed my latest God venture. As we were laughing at the events that God arranged, Amy stopped and said, *"I think you should write a book about your stories."* BAM! Two signs in one day and only hours apart. Her words registered deep in my heart. Within the week another friend, Bob, suggested I put all my experiences in a book. More signs kept coming. I realized that I was supposed to write a book regardless of my literary skills.

This was a monumental task for me, and my frustration grew every time I tried to put words on paper. I searched for any reason to quit and every obstacle justified my cause to give up. God however, simply opened another door and kept the project moving forward.

I knew virtually nothing about the book business, so I asked God how we would get the book published. The next day I received a postcard from a printing company in Naples, Florida, addressed to me stating, *"We will help you publish and print your book."* There was no logical explanation of how that company got my name. I had only shared God's request with a few close friends.

It took a few years to complete a rough draft, and I needed to locate an editor. I asked God who He had in mind. Within days, a friend working on his doctorate randomly recommended an editor if I ever needed one, and I knew this was God. My book took this editor by surprise because it was very different from the work she had done in the past. She confided in me that she recently asked God to let her edit some Christian materials instead of only doctorial theses. God amazingly answered both of our prayers at the same time. She provided me with excellent advice on how to move forward and clean up the book. Throughout the entire project God conveniently brought all the pieces and people together. Without His direction, help, and encouragement this would never have happened. It was all God!

God was persistent. While it seemed an insurmountable task at the beginning, I came to enjoy sitting down and putting these events into words. What if God asked you to do something you were not qualified to do? Would you do it?

> God is more concerned with your availability than your lack of ability.

I knew I did not possess the skills when God asked me to go into the prisons, to be a pastor, or even write this book. At first, I ignored the signs, but God quickly taught me that it was not about my abilities, only my obedience. God's requests are based on His love for us, not our qualifications. Once we make ourselves available He sends us the strength and the resources to take care of everything else

Peter never possessed the ability to walk on water, but as soon as he was willing to step out of the boat, Jesus supplied the power. You just need to have enough courage to put your leg over the side of the boat and take that first step. God loves to see us walk in the unknown because it encourages our faith. Ask God to give you the ability to recognize His presence in your life, then watch and see what He does.

"Father, you said you would never leave me nor forsake me, but sometimes I struggle with the idea that all circumstances are designed for my good. Speak to me in a way I will understand. Give me the eyes to see you working and the ears to hear your leading. I ask this in the name of your son, Jesus."

Relax, God will begin to speak. You may see it today, or it may take several days to discover what God is saying. Just be patient and never give up.

Task at Hand

Think of last time you used the word coincidence. Ask God if it was Him and see what He says.

_____

_____

_____

_____

_____

_____

When we see God working in every situation, we realize our lives have purpose.

Helpful Biblical Principle

For the eyes of the Lord search back and forth across the whole earth, looking for people whose hearts are perfect toward Him, so that He can show His great power in helping them.

2 Chronicles 16:9   TLB

- *Chapter Six* -

Author of Our Faith

"Building faith through life's circumstances"

Winning with God

Once you establish a connection with God and become familiar with His voice, life takes on greater breadth. You become gifted to make each moment in your life count for so much more. Each day presents you with the possibility of living bigger than the day before. Exposure to God's presence causes a change in you that is so amazing that others will stand up and take notice.

God knows your potential and has already set into motion a series of events that will mature the nature He has hidden within you. God loves you the way you are, but He is unwavering in His pursuit to form you into the person He destined you to be.

Once I understood this idea, I realized God was actually using all the circumstances in my life to allow me the chance to experience Him. The closer we became as friends, the faster I began to develop His character. Anything I encountered in life had the potential to mature me. I was beginning to see that God's grace was boundless. He possesses the power to draw the good out of every situation. In the right light, I could now see how each event was actually forming an awareness in me of God's continual presence. I no longer needed to figure out my problem; I just needed to focus on God and watch what He would do. The more I set my eyes on God, the easier it became to meet life's challenges, and the more my faith grew.

> God possesses the power to draw the good out of every situation.

The Bible tells us how important faith is.

And without faith it is impossible to please God, because anyone who comes to Him must believe that He exists and that He rewards those who earnestly seek Him.

Hebrews 11:6 NIV

Faith is what actually pleases God. Walking by faith means you will have to trust in an unseen God. You do this by becoming sensitive to His invisible presence working in and around your life. The Bible clearly reveals that God will never be seen by the naked eye (1John 4:12). That great event will only take place after you are released from this earthly body. This means if you are going to walk with God you have to go by way of the Spirit and rely less on what you see. Relinquishing your trust in the tangible and becoming confident in the spiritual is not an easy task. To help you along this path, God permits circumstances in your life that allow Him to reveal the power He has placed within you. Just as a window allows you to enjoy the benefits of the sun and wind, your faith gives you access to the resources of God's Kingdom in the here and now.

God is deeply concerned about every aspect of your life, so each circumstance, whether good or bad, is merely an opportunity for God to get involved. God's presence makes the impossible possible (Matthew 19:26). Your birth was only the first chapter in a story of success. Your involvement, however, will allow it to stand out as a footnote in history. The ending is up to you.

God has allowed difficult times to grace my life, but He was not the originator of them. The bone disease and heart attack were direct results of my decisions and life situations. God was not out to harm, hinder, or punish me in any way. I was doing a good enough job of that myself. Even when life took a terrible turn, God stepped in and brought forth a blessing from what seemed like a curse. No matter where our choices take us, God's intention for our lives can never be restricted by our present circumstances. He can always move us forward, no matter what.

We can see this truth plainly in the lives of Joseph and Moses. Both men were sent by God to rescue His people. Joseph's calling was to save his family from an impending drought years in the future. During his youth Joseph's brothers became jealous of their father's love for him and secretly sold him into slavery. But God stepped in and turned his life of hardships into one of great honor. Joseph became a powerful leader in a new land with God's guidance, and opened the doors to deliver his family as promised. Joseph acknowledged that what his brothers meant for evil God worked out for good (Genesis 39–47).

Generations later the Israelites were forced into hard labor, and God raised up Moses to deliver them from their slavery. God miraculously placed him within Pharaoh's family to bring freedom to His people. As a young man, Moses got side tracked when he discovered he was not Egyptian, and in an attempt to protect a fellow Israelite, killed one of Pharaoh's guards. Pharaoh issued a decree of death over Moses, and he was forced to leave Egypt. He hid in the land of Midian for forty years, but his calling never changed. God just altered the scenario by speaking through a burning bush to encourage Moses to return to Egypt and get His plan back on track. Moses' return to Egypt brought about a great victory for God's people (Exodus 2-13).

> God is never restricted by the circumstances our choices put us in. He just gets more creative.

We can see that when life looked hopeless in both of these men's lives, God simply turned every problem into a blessing. God's goodness allows Him to use even our present predicaments to develop tomorrow's victories.

Building faith and trusting in God takes time and patience. The reason that God does not remove every obstacle in your life is that without a problem He cannot reveal Himself to you as problem solver. To explain this further I need to go back to the Book of Exodus in the Bible.

God's name is actually not "God." This is a man-made label and it simply means, "Self sufficient one." That is to say, God requires no one or nothing else to exist. God gave a better description of Himself when He spoke to Moses through the burning bush. Moses asked, *"Who shall I say sent me?"* God responded, *"I am that I am."* (Exodus 3:14) It was at this moment God enlightened Moses of the fact that He was capable of being whatever Moses needed. *I am* your deliverer, *I am* your healer, *I am* your strength, *I am* your protector; whatever you need me to be, I will be. This response birthed the name of Jehovah, "The Lord," to which the Israelites added endings such as Jehovah Shalom, *"The Lord our peace,"* or Jehovah Rophi, *"The Lord who heals you,"* and others. Each time they witnessed God's faithfulness they added another name to their list.

As situations arise we need to learn to focus not on the crisis, but on the answer: *God.* Our greatest confession about God is declaring to others what He has brought us through. Living by faith means to live a life without worry. You rest in the knowledge that God has a plan in every circumstance to bring you through, stronger and wiser. Now you can face life with the knowledge that He is there and ready to help. Faith then becomes an action rather than a thought process. Let me share with you a few stories that helped build my faith, opened my eyes, and allowed me to add a new name to my list.

Do It Again

One day as I was encouraging a coworker, Alan, by telling him about the benefits of knowing God, he cut the conversation short and excused himself. Alan said he was beginning to see halos around the lights and that signaled the beginning of another terrible migraine. He wanted to get home before the headache made it difficult to drive. As he turned to leave something rose up in me that I had never experienced. Before I realized it, I had grabbed a hold of Alan's shoulder and began praying. *"In Jesus' name, be healed!"* I told Alan to watch the clock and remember the exact time he felt the headache leave as he drove home. I turned and left without giving him a chance to respond. Back in my office I tried to go over my reasoning for such blunt behavior. I was stunned at what I had done and a nervousness got the best of me for a few hours. I wondered if I had been too forward with him.

By the next morning I had forgotten the entire incident. I was back at work getting ready for the day when Alan showed up in my office shouting, *"three-fifteen."* I was clueless, but he just kept saying, *"three-fifteen."* I asked him to clarify and he stated that this was the time on his car radio when he realized his headache was completely gone. Alan was ecstatic because he had never encountered such a rapid change in his headaches. Normally he would be couch ridden for hours, and sometimes days. I was amazed at how prompt the Lord was in healing Alan.

A couple of days later Alan located me in the hallway and stated, *"Do it again! Do it again!"* over and over. I got a little nervous because I had no idea what he was trying to ask me and at the same time he was literally dragging me to the men's bathroom. Once we were inside the men's room I finally understood. *"The headache thing, you know. Do it again!"* Alan needed God's assistance. Despite the surroundings we prayed and off he went. Later, Alan stopped by to confess that he felt much better and was only dealing with a minor headache. Earlier, he was worried that if his headache did not subside he would have to leave work. He was grateful, but I told him it was entirely the Lord's doing and that he should thank Him. He agreed.

It amazed me how quickly Alan's trust grew in God's goodness. After only one small healing he was ready to ask for more. You could see his faith growing. Today I am totally convinced God can heal, but the method is up to Him. I have witnessed plenty of miracles since then, and each time my trust in God's kind nature grows a little stronger.

An Amazing Transformation

Lunch time was a great opportunity to share my God experiences, and this is where I got to know Melissa. She approached me one winter and asked if we could agree in prayer for her daughter. Sherry had received a closed-head injury in an accident, and the complications were making it difficult for her to perform normal, everyday tasks. We drew up a list of the things that needed to change in Sherry's mental and physical health that would enable her to lead a normal life. We prayed for Sherry's recovery, and as the year progressed she began to show some improvement. Months passed, and Fall arrived again when I found our prayer list inside the pocket of my winter coat. I showed Melissa our list and inquired about Sherry's condition. She happily exclaimed that every request we had put before the Lord either had been fulfilled or was showing improvement. We were encouraged and continued to pray for Sherry.

One afternoon I knew it was time to ask God to completely restore Sherry so she could lead a productive normal life. Melissa felt God was leading her in the same direction, so we agreed in prayer and watched the Lord go right back to work. Day after day we would swap more stories about what God was doing in each other's lives and discuss Sherry's progress. Soon others were stopping by to hear what was going on, and we started praying for their lives as well. God was meeting so many needs, and it was wonderful to see the level of faith growing in so many people.

Sherry was under the care of multiple specialists and each prescribed a medication for his or her particular treatment. Even with some noticeable side effects the doctors felt the medications were necessary. Sherry was continuing to do better, so we prayed that the doctors would consider reducing her prescriptions. Soon after our prayer Sherry developed a cancerous tumor on her thyroid. At first, we felt like our prayers were being ignored, but we soon learned that the doctor treating the cancer requested that all other medications be either reduced or eliminated to make sure his tests were not compromised. We realized God was answering our requests in a unique way. This solved the excessive medication issue, so now we could focus our attention on the cancer.

> At times when I felt confident in God's faithfulness, He would take me to the edge of my faith and show me there was still more to be learned.

Melissa had gone through so many struggles that her faith was beginning to diminish. She was noticeably distraught about Sherry's cancer, so we prayed that God would give us clear direction about what He was doing. God was quick to respond. During a drive downtown Melissa had stopped at a red light and without warning or explanation her car lurched forward and rear-ended an expensive Cadillac. She thought someone hit her from behind, but there was no one in the rear view mirror and her foot was still firmly planted on the brake. Melissa's heart sank. She felt as if life was going from bad to worse. Her plate was too full from her daughter's medical issues to deal with an accident.

With tear-filled eyes she approached the other vehicle. Instead of the usual name and license swapping, the driver emerged from her car and exclaimed this accident should have never happened. The driver of the Cadillac told Melissa that she always puts in a request to God for an angel whenever she takes to the road and they have never failed her, so something must be wrong. The lady remarked, *"There must be a reason for God to allow this mishap."* She looked straight at Melissa and asked if there was something wrong with her family. This brought on another flood of tears and out came the story of Sherry's situation. The lady was convinced that this was the reason for the accident. She insisted that they pray for Melissa's daughter on the spot. After they prayed she told Melissa that she was on her way to church and assured her that the entire congregation would pray for her situation as well. Then, to their amazement they inspected their cars and found no damage, not even a scratch. The other driver got in her car and drove away, leaving Melissa speechless.

This renewed Melissa's faith. She was confident that God was on her side and would help her face this most recent battle. We prayed for the cancer to be removed, and God sent a wonderful surgeon. The report came back that the cancer was so well contained there should be no further problems. God is still restoring Sherry. Her focus and motor skills are improving, helping her lead a more normal life! This miracle did not work itself out in a few seconds; instead, God chose to do it over time and through the use of doctors. Even when cancer attacked, God was able to use it to solve another problem, and then He healed the cancer as well. God is not done with Sherry; she is continuing to recover and we see small victories everyday. Melissa has become a powerful believer, and she continually encourages everyone to put their trust in God's faithfulness. Where does your trust lie?

At times when I felt confident in God's faithfulness He would take me to the edge of my faith to show me there was more to be learned. I will admit that I really struggle at those times in my life, because peace and patience seem to be in short supply. But they have always been rewarding in the end. Just like my next story.

Thirty-Second Knee Replacement

During the summer I run a small side business, and as the season was drawing to a close my knees began to ache. One knee became so sore that I needed to wear a brace to get through the day. There was no obvious reason for the pain since I never injured the knee, so I thought this would go away if I pampered it. The pain only intensified, and my wife suggested I go see a doctor. *"Let me see what God wants me to do,"* was my natural response. After spending some time with God, I felt He was telling me not to go.

I muddled through the next four months without any improvement in my knee. There were times when I became so impatient that I was determined to see a doctor, and each time I went to make an appointment God made it quite clear He did not want me to go. I have to admit that this incident tested my obedience. Rationally, I felt I should see a doctor, but there was something in my heart that knew that I could trust God, so I waited patiently.

One day a friend randomly suggested that I attend a men's retreat for some encouragement. Work was busy and our children's activities demanded lots of time. He felt I needed to get away and spend some quiet time with God. I shared this suggestion with my friend Mike at church. Oddly enough, he got the same suggestion from someone he knew. Mike found some information on a retreat a few hours away, but he was lacking the funds. Traveling together would be a great idea, so we asked God for confirmation. We also brought the idea before our wives to see what they thought. God opened the door to go, because not only did both our wives agree, my wife felt we should pay for Mike's costs so that I would not have to travel alone.

The retreat was an amazing experience. Everywhere we turned God was answering questions, giving us direction, and totally astounding us. During the second service of the retreat, the minister believed God wanted to heal people in the audience with arthritic knees. I decided not to stand up because I did not think the problem in my knee was due to arthritis. I felt I was too young, but I was ready to move if he mentioned any other knee problems. Instead, he prayed for those that stood up, and then quickly moved on into his message. At that moment I thought I missed God and my chance for a healing. Quietly I prayed and apologized to the Lord for missing His call. Immediately, both my knees began to feel warm and I could tell something was different. Wandering to the back of the auditorium I found a place and tried to kneel. The muscles felt tight, but there were no sharp pains as I knelt down. I could not believe the difference, so I tried it a few more times and was overwhelmed at how good my knees felt.

Back at the hotel I showed Mike the change by kneeling on the floor. He agreed it had to be a miracle. After a few weeks of stretching, my knees felt completely normal, and I returned to my normal tasks without any problems. God gave me a total knee replacement that day in thirty seconds. I guess He was trying to teach me patience. Now I am more confident in God's faithfulness, but it is His timing I still have to get used to.

We all need to learn more about who God is. The problem we encounter in this task is that we hold on to the opinions of our family and friends too strongly. Some are right, but some are also wrong. You and God need to work that out. All I know is if you want to go farther and see more of God, you have to let go of something. If the God you believe in does not have the power to change your life it may be time to find a new one. My stories may encourage you, but it is only a personal experience that can build your faith.

The point I am trying to make is that the events in our lives provide perfect opportunities to get to know God better and allow Him the chance to help us in limitless ways. God is a healer, a supplier, a stress reliever, a strengthener, a friend, or whatever you need because He is the great *I Am!* Just give it over to God and see how He handles the matter. Get Him involved in your life and add another name to your list. We cannot grow in faith

> God is obsessed with us living a victorious life.

without a challenge. Difficult situations allow us to witness a new dimension of God. Faith is not positive thinking that hopes God will get involved, it is a lifestyle that draws God to us and makes great things happen.

Jesus turned and saw her. "Take heart, daughter," he said, "your faith has healed you." And the woman was healed from that moment. (emphasis mine)

Matthew 9:22 NIV

Then he touched their eyes and said, "According to your faith will it be done to you"; and their sight was restored. (emphasis mine)

Matthew 9:29-30 NIV

It is <u>not</u> acceptable to be disappointed with God when we encounter tough circumstances in our lives. We must stop asking Him *why?* and start asking, "*What can I learn from this situation and how can I get you (God) involved?*" This will revolutionize your life. He is obsessed with you living a victorious life. His wisdom is beyond logic, and His purpose is too vast for our rational minds to comprehend. Yet, all His ways are perfect.

Begin your walk of faith by taking one small step and writing in the following space where you would like some help, and then step out to meet Him. These are the actions of faith that please God and prompt Him to work upon your behalf. His faithfulness makes it impossible for Him to let us down. As our opening scripture on faith tells us: God rewards those who earnestly seek Him (Hebrews 11:6). Everyone needs to see God work in their life at least one time. What can God do to help you believe in Him more?

Note:
The greatest step of faith is to hand your life over to God. This important decision will open your eyes to the presence of God and fill your heart with the courage to believe. Turn back to page 19 and make that commitment today!

Task at Hand

First, recognize that every struggle is just a new
    chance to experience God.
Second, think about a problem and ask God to show
    you what He is doing to help you.
Third, ask God what you can do to help Him.
Fourth, write down what you see and hear.

_____

_____

_____

_____

_____

_____

_____

_____

_____

_____

_____

_____

_____

_____

_____

God will be our protector, our provider, our strength, our healer, our everything! <u>If</u> we let Him.

Helpful Biblical Principles

And we know that in all things God works for the good of those who love him, who have been called according to his purpose.

Romans 8:28 NIV

Let us fix our eyes on Jesus, the author and perfecter of our faith.

Hebrews 12:2 NIV

- *Chapter Seven* -

Great Expectations

"Taking our limitations off of God"

Great Expectations

Up to this point, my idea of God could be easily simplified into a few basic rules. Go to church occasionally, sing a few songs, give some loose change, and within an hour I was back to more exciting activities. Things got even easier once I reduced my commitment down to only Christmas and Easter, because I thought God could be simply adjusted to fit my lifestyle.

Now I was beginning to see a whole new side of God. He had something to say, places to go, and things to do. There was a lot more to Him than I realized. He offered me a new life, not one made up of following rules, but one based on a real relationship. We were communicating, and I could see that I needed to spend more time with God if I wanted to know Him better.

I discovered there were lots of benefits to hanging around God and I sensed that He enjoyed being with me just as much. God was not as hard to find as I once thought. The reason He is so accessible is because He removed all the barriers that once separated us. It was never in God's plan to be apart from man, so He created a place where He could always reach us, touch us, bless us, and speak to us all the time. He placed us in His son, Jesus; because in Him there is nothing, not even sin, standing in God's way (Ephesians 1:3).

If God's love is no longer hindered, why not experiment with it? He is Jehovah Jireh, "The Lord who provides." Ask God to provide you with an experience that will build your faith in Him. Put no limits or parameters on your request. *"Lord, do it your way and in your timing."* Then sit back and look to see what happens. Based on my past experiences something is bound to take place. These consistent interventions of God have taken me to great levels of faith. My desire now is that God would be involved in every area of my life. Today, when I ask, I have great expectations that God will show up. Doubt is no longer acceptable (James 1:6). I will admit that I was not always this positive that every situation would work out. Trusting in God will seem risky, but the rewards are worth it. When God steps out of the background and works in the realm of the miraculous, everything changes. Nothing will be insignificant to us any longer. We will see people and circumstances with a new mental and spiritual attitude.

> In Jesus Christ nothing stands in God's way, not even sin.

The ability to give generously is an attitude I have tried to cultivate. There is no greater way to impact another person's life than to meet a need. Our money, time, and talents can make a powerful difference in someone's life. God has always taken care of my family, so whenever possible we like to lend a hand. We cannot out give God, but it sure is fun to try. This is a story of how I got to reap what I had been sowing.

Godly Provision

My wife and I were sitting around discussing the merits of a treadmill. We decided it would be a nice addition, but our finances were depleted. Constant giving and unforeseen bills did not allow us to have the savings available for this kind of purchase. Not to mention, we were supporting four wonderful children and all their activities. I had the faith that God could provide if we simply asked. We were not asking for a large amount, and since I never approached God with a "gimme" mind-set I was confident that the Lord would provide a way.

We agreed five hundred dollars should cover the cost, so I started a short prayer asking God to provide the way for us to purchase a treadmill. After making the request I ended the discussion and excused myself, but not without saying we should expect the money shortly. I felt a strange feeling of boldness, and it showed in my attitude. It was as though I knew that God would get the money to us somehow.

The very next day I found Geralynn with our friend, Kathy, at the kitchen table having a unique conversation. They were sliding an envelope back and forth across the table. Kathy was demanding that my wife take it, and my wife would slide it back, stating we would not. I interrupted and asked what the discussion was about. Geralynn piped up and said that Kathy was trying to give us some money, which was in the envelope being passed around. I learned that the amount was five hundred dollars, which was not a surprise.

I tend to get a little excited when I see God working, so I humorously asked Geralynn if she remembered our conversation from the night before and she quickly told me, *"Be Quiet!"* This was way too good to let go, so I asked her again and got an even better response: *"Not now! Shut up!"* I should have stopped asking questions, but I was having way too much fun. Geralynn was uncomfortable with Kathy giving us so much money, even though it was exactly what we prayed for. My wife was right, and we both knew she could not afford such an amount. She had a growing small business, but this sum of money would definitely impact her budget.

I asked Kathy to elaborate on how God brought this matter to her attention. The previous evening she felt she had received some specific signs from God that she was supposed to give us some money. She had no problems giving us money, it was the amount that made her a little nervous. As she hesitated doubt set in, so she called my sister to see if something was wrong. My sister could not verify any financial difficulties, so Kathy decided the idea was not from God and tried to let it go. The next morning a friend from church called. Kathy's friend had been in prayer and felt God wanted to give her a message. *"God wants you to do whatever He put on our heart."* Kathy was stunned because she had not told anyone what she was thinking of doing. That phone call was all she needed, and now she was convinced God was in on the whole thing. Kathy told us, *"I was so freaked by the call that I drove to the bank as fast as I could and demanded they give me five hundred dollars right now. I couldn't get the money fast enough."*

I looked at Geralynn and said, *"Take the money. We don't want to rob her of a blessing!"* My wife knew I was right, and with a little reluctance we took the money. We helped Kathy understand what was happening by telling her our side of the story and about our prayer to purchase a treadmill. She was relieved that she had heard correctly and was not just making it all up. Kathy was excited that she was able to be obedient to God. However, our feelings about the money had changed as we realized the importance of it. This was not just five hundred dollars; it was a gift from God through a dear friend. We did not want to squander it on a treadmill because the money was from Kathy's budget and not her savings.

We decided the best thing to do was to sow it into someone else's life. We asked God to open a door and within a few days He put someone with a greater need than ours before us. The money was a powerful blessing to these people. We were certain God would multiply this money again, and He has. God is simply the greatest provider of all. The money was God's anyway; in fact, everything we think we "own" is really God's. By the way, we finally did get that treadmill; it just took a couple of years and we really enjoy it.

I ran into Kathy later and mentioned the money. She laughed and said it was one of the hardest things she had ever done. Kathy knew she could not pay all her bills once she gave us the money, but she was determined to obey God. To make matters worse just days after she gave us the money she lost a large account that made her financial situation appear even worse. Kathy stayed confident that the Lord would meet her needs because she was obedient. God did show up and turned her financial situation completely around. She got three new large accounts that brought in more money than the one she lost. Her business is still prospering and growing today. Kathy admitted she has never made so much money. She still believes that without the chance to sow that money into our lives she would have never seen this change in her financial situation.

> God has acknowledged in His word that He is for you _not_ against you.

God sometimes asks us to do things that may seem impossible, but there is always a purpose. We just need to find the courage to step out as Kathy did. Remember, we can never ruin God's plan if we decide not to do to what He is asking of us. Actually, we just hinder ourselves by robbing God of the chance to bless us in return. Think about it.

I always thought God was too busy to get involved in the details of my life so I usually tried to limit my requests to only larger issues. Since we were on friendlier terms I decided to see if He wanted to help out more often. I discovered that God was just waiting to get involved with everything I had going on. The next story shows all I had to do was ask. This situation also helped me understand why my mom always told me, *"Be nice to everyone— you never know where you will see them again."*

Be Nice to Strangers

After completing a rather large job, I had not received payment in over a month, so I stopped by to make sure everything was all right. Max, the person who scheduled the job, commented that the owner was disappointed with my work and was not going to pay. I thought Max was the owner of the business and as we discussed the matter I began to realize he truly *was* the owner. I tried to resolve all the issues, but he would simply create a new one to explain why He should not have to pay. I finally gave up and told Max that if it was on his heart not to pay, then that was his choice. Max got furious about the heart comment saying that I could not know what was on his heart. I was concerned by Max's angry reaction, so I excused myself and left. I decided it was time to drop the issue.

On the way home I told the Lord that if He ever made Max pay I would use the money to bless someone else. If God could get money from someone like that, He could have it! I actually did not expect to ever see the money.

Well, God must have wanted the money because He immediately went to work. That same day my sister, Karen, called to see how I was doing. I told her what had just happened, and she asked a strange question, one that changed the entire situation. She asked me if the owner's name was Max, because she had a friend, Jackie, whose husband owned the same type of business. I was shocked! Karen knew Max personally. She informed me that we were also attending the same church as Max and Jackie and at that moment I knew God was going to do something big. I just did not realize how big.

We were new to the church and had not met everyone, but I felt the next Sunday was going to be quite interesting. Sunday came and I met Jackie, but Max was not in attendance. I never mentioned what happened, so I just prayed for Max and her because I knew God would show me what to do when the time came. In the meantime God was using the situation to get more people involved. David, my friend, had a brother who needed some help roofing his house, so I offered to pitch in, and we scheduled a time. The job turned out to be larger than we expected, so David and his brother arranged to have more of their family help the following day. David began to list all his family members who would be helping us, and when he mentioned Jackie's name I lost my breath. Then he mentioned that her husband, Max, would also be stopping by to lend a hand. I had never realized they were all related.

I could not believe it. Tomorrow Max and I would be face to face again. Our last meeting had not gone so well, and I was not looking forward to a repeat in front of David's family. After I told David and his brother the entire story I decided to excuse myself from roofing in order to keep the peace. But they just laughed and said he does that kind of stuff all the time. In fact, they were really excited to see what would happen. David begged me to return the next day and even though I had a very uneasy feeling, I agreed.

The next day there were more people at the house than I remembered hearing about. I learned later that David had called the rest of his family to tell them what was going on, and everyone wanted to be there to see what would happen. Roofing was now secondary. I did not want Max to recognize me, so I kept my hat pulled down to my nose and my face towards the roof. It did not help when David's brother began to tell everyone how blessed they were to have me there. Soon everyone wanted to meet me. My goal, however, was to stay on the roof all day and never get down except to run to my car and leave. The moment I ran out of nails I asked David to get me a fresh supply; he just smiled and said, "*No.*" Nice friend. He wanted me off the roof and into the mix of people below. I was almost back to the ladder when Max and I exchanged glances. He walked straight over and told me that he had recently learned that Karen, who was a friend of his wife's, was also my sister. He apologized for the exchange at his business and told me, "*You can stop over next week and pick up your check.*"

As I approached the top of the ladder, I found everybody had stopped working because they were eagerly waiting to hear every detail of our conversation. I went back to work and ignored them for as long as possible, then I finally explained how we worked everything out and resolved the matter.

Remember, *"Be nice to everyone— you never know where you will see them again."*

Oh, and the money? Not surprisingly, God revealed a need as fast as the money touched my hands, and that was fine with me. Just to see God bring good out of that entire situation made it worth every cent. Everyone in David's family was blessed by the outcome, and realized that God has the ability to turn any difficult situation into a blessing. I was just excited to be a part of it, and now I just expect it to happen.

Over-Balanced Checkbook

My summer business was coming to a close, and I wanted to financially bless a few friends. With a few jobs completed and payments on the way, I decided to write some checks then deposit the money before they were cashed. These checks definitely exceeded the balance in our business account, but we had overdraft protection. With that in mind I knew there was enough in savings to cover everything.

A few days later we received some checks, and I noticed that the business account still had a positive balance even before the deposit. I assumed everything went as planned, and we beat the checks to the bank. However, a week later the bank statement arrived and gave us a different story. It showed that same positive balance, amazingly all the checks *had* been cashed before I went to the bank. We looked over the business records and confirmed that our balance should have been a deficit. We contacted the bank, but everything was satisfactory with them. We could not find where the money came from, so we finally gave up and decided God cashed those checks for us at no charge.

Some of you may think it is strange to test God's word, but I believe He wants us to try it out. Testing His word in faith, after all, is not the same as doubting it. God has released a lot of great promises because of Jesus' hard work, and He does not want all of His sacrifice to go to waste.

> If God wants to bless us, then we are obligated to give Him every opportunity possible.

If putting the Bible to work does not fit into your God box, try out this verse:

> *Bring the whole tithe into the storehouse, that there may be food in my house. Test me in this," says the LORD Almighty, "and see if I will not throw open the floodgates of heaven and pour out so much blessing that you will not have room enough for it. (emphasis mine)*

Malachi 3:10-11 NIV

If God wants to bless us, then we are obligated to give Him every opportunity possible. You can read my stories, or you can experience them yourself. Jesus' sacrifice brought heaven and earth back together. In heaven, it moved God from a position of judgment to a place of grace and mercy, so as far as God is concerned, we are totally forgiven. Now, all His blessings are just waiting to be released to whoever desires them. The moment we accept Jesus' sacrifice, God has all the freedom to touch any area of our life here on earth. Allow Him to help you understand who He is and how great His love is toward you. Today, God will never be closer to anyone else than He is to you. He will not answer anyone quicker than He will answer you. He is now your God and personal friend. Jesus' sacrifice was a perfect work, and that is the good news.

God is able to work everything out for the best, but you must be willing to let Him work in your life. One of the greatest prayers you can compose is simply asking for *"Help!"* Give Him the chance to do something for you and expect Him to show up. God has declared He is willing to live in our hearts and you can not get any closer than that. Each time you experience God's presence you will be propelled to a new level of great expectation. God acknowledged in His word He is for you and not against you (Romans 8:31).

Task at Hand

Decide today how you are going to give God the opportunity to get involved in your life.

- Opportunity -

_____

_____

_____

_____

_____

_____

- SIGNS -

_____

_____

_____

_____

_____

_____

_____

As we give God our struggles and become free of their weight, we align ourselves to receive His endless blessings.

Helpful Biblical Principle

Do not be deceived: God cannot be mocked. A man reaps what he sows. The one who sows to please his sinful nature, from that nature will reap destruction; the one who sows to please the Spirit, from the Spirit will reap eternal life. Let us not become weary in doing good, for at the proper time we will reap a harvest if we do not give up.

Galatians 6:7-9 NIV

Chapter Eight

Benefits

"Obedience rewards us with the abundant life."

Walking with God definitely has its benefits. What amazes me about Him is that He is willing to supply us with all the resources to encourage and build up others; then He actually turns around and rewards us for accomplishing the tasks He gave us. Let me give you an analogy to help you understand what I mean. When I was young my parents would give me an extra allowance at Christmas so I could buy gifts for them. In essence they were supplying the money for their own presents.

God works in the same fashion. He created me to do good works (Ephesians 2:10). He then placed the desire in me to want to see that these deeds are completed (Philippians 2:13). Then He supplies all the resources and abilities to complete these tasks (Isaiah 26:12). Finally, once the work is done, God blesses me for doing what He actually designed and empowered me to do because His law of reaping and sowing demands it (Galatians 6:7-9). This is what the Bible calls the abundant life, a life of perpetual increase. Our trust in God starts this sequence of events, and even this first step of trust is God's work (Ephesians 2:8). I discovered this concept in the most surprising ways.

The Golf Tournament

Geralynn and I were attending a conference in Texas put together by our Bishop. This was one of the few trips we had taken together without the children. During a break in the four-day schedule, we decided to tour the Dallas area and take in the sights. However, it was highly recommended that I attend a golf outing sponsored by the Bishop. I tried to get out of it, but Geralynn pointed out that the words "should attend" really meant "must attend." Geralynn graciously agreed to remain at the hotel with our friend Maria while her husband, Alex, accompanied me on the golf outing. Attending the Bishop's fundraiser was a good idea, but it was not the highest on my list of things I wanted to do on our mini-vacation. After a little encouragement from my wife, I put the whole day in God's hands and decided to make the best of it.

> God is not looking for talent, just obedience.

I had only golfed once before. It was not pretty, and my golf skills had not changed much since then. Our lack of equipment, skills, and lingo made us the team to avoid. We needed four people to enter the scramble and even the last pair refused to join us. Just before teeing off we acquired one more person so that we had the minimum three people we needed to participate. Let me tell you, this guy was the man of the hour: he had the shoes, the clubs and even the talk to back it up. I was impressed, and hopefully my jeans, tennis shoes, and questions about how to drive the golf cart did not give me away as a novice.

I made the best of it and took in the beautiful scenery of the course. I will not go into the details of the entire eighteen holes, but we began to notice something extraordinary around the fourth hole. Our third man, Mark, ended up being a remarkable golfer. His drives, chips and putting shaved numerous strokes from our score. To my amazement, whenever Mark missed his shot, either Alex or I would make a valiant effort, placing us close to the hole or onto the green. I actually put us inches from the cup more than once. I have experienced a few events that I can not explain, but our golfing that day was nothing short of miraculous. One seventy-five yard worm burner rolled down the fairway, onto the green and then bounced off the cup. Another shot went into the woods, ricocheted off more than one tree and bounced out onto the green. Random sacrificial putts used to find the lay of the green found their way to the bottom of the hole. We consistently got one or two under par, which I'm told is a birdie and eagle, respectively (Sorry golfers, I am still learning). After a few more amazing 40-foot putts, we returned to the clubhouse for final tallies and awards.

The results were in and before any awards were dispensed, the Bishop wanted to inform us of a miracle that had occurred on the course. I scanned the room for someone who may have experienced some form of physical healing at the conference the night before. Instead, we were informed that the miracle was our team taking second place in the tournament. The Bishop told everyone he almost teamed up with Alex and me because he felt sorry for us, but he decided to golf with one of the speakers from the conference instead. He felt that the minister's powerful anointing would give them an advantage over the other teams and put them into a winning position.

I do not know how a two-time golfer gets second place, but I was shocked. The ride home was one filled with laughter and amazement. We decided to leave our trophies in the car and told our wives that we had taken second place. I was confident of Geralynn's response. *"Yeah right!"* she laughed and Maria's reaction was almost the same. The realization that we were telling the truth did not materialize until they noticed our trophies buckled up in the back seat—for safety reasons of course.

We laughed about that one all the way home. The trophy still sits on my night stand to remind me that God still works miracles and that He rewards us for the needs of others before our own.

Too many times I try to use my limited knowledge to understand what God is up to, and every time my mind gets involved I end up even more confused than before. God has taught me that our friendship is actually a matter of the heart. It is more important to trust what is in my heart than what is in my head. God gave me an excellent advisor to assist me in living out of my heart, His Holy Spirit. The day I accepted Christ into my heart (not my head) I was given my own personal aide, someone who would be with me all the days of my life.

He would be...

- a teacher   Luke 12:12
- a counselor   John 14:26
- a guide to truth   John 16:13
- a warning system   Acts 20:23
- a source of power   Acts 1:8
- a revealer of God's intent   1Corinth 9-10
- without limit   John 3:34

These are just a few of the many benefits we receive when God's Spirit dwells in us. God is the master of turning bad situations into victories as I discovered in the next story.

Baltimore and Back

A friend of mine moved to Baltimore to pastor a small inner city church. The neighborhood was quite poor and he did not have much to work with so God began encouraging me to visit him. Traveling out of state and working in the streets of a big city was way out of my comfort zone at that time. Once I became confident that God was leading me in that direction I asked my friend, David, to go with me. If he was able to go, I would take that as a sign that I was on the right track; besides a partner would make the task easier. David always liked a good God adventure, but he was not sure if his job would let him go, so he was quite surprised when they gave him the time off.

With my first confirmation out of the way, I asked the Lord to verify if this was the proper time to go. I got my reply when we visited a small church near our cabin in Northern Michigan. The church was sponsoring a visiting speaker for the week.

We had heard some of his tapes, so we were excited to see him in person. The night we went he shared a story that was very similar to my situation.

God told the speaker to travel to Ireland and sing praise songs in the streets. Kind of a strange request, but he agreed and began to share his desire to go to Ireland with the churches he visited. Within a few short weeks, $1200 in contributions came from people who wanted to help sponsor his trip. He decided to call and price a round trip ticket, which of course was exactly $1200. He knew this was a confirmation and not a coincidence, so he scheduled the flight and left with no itinerary except hotel arrangements.

In Ireland, he began to doubt his word from God because he found no open door for public ministry. Each day he wandered the streets trying to find some glimpse of God but instead he only befriended a blind couple he met in a small shopping square. The couple's only source of income was singing love songs in public for donations. Every time they met he simply spoke about God's love for them and within days they surrendered their lives to Jesus. With only one day left He had still not accomplished what the God had sent him to do. He spent the last evening with his new friends and they made one final request: they asked the speaker to sing with them in the market on his last day in Ireland. That day, God faithfully opened the door for him to sing worship songs in public with thousands of on-lookers.

> When you are not sure of what God wants, it is better to step out than to stand still.

Pleased with how things turned out, he returned home, but on his flight back he learned that it was illegal in Ireland to conduct any religious activity in public because of a newly enacted law. Immediately he realized that God not only opened up a door to sing Christian music publicly, but He also left behind a blind couple, that would be able to continue singing God's praises publicly. No one with a good conscience would jail a blind couple who were loved by the community and whose only source of income was performing public concerts. In conclusion to his story the speaker stated, *"God still speaks to people and when they listen he opens the door to accomplish all that He asks."* This was what God had been teaching me.

The parallel between this minister's journey and my calling to go to the streets of Baltimore was too *"perfect"*. I knew this was no coincidence, so during prayer that night I told God I knew He wanted me to go, and this service was a confirmation. I did not like to step out until I had three signs to verify my assignment, so I could hardly wait to see the next confirmation because, without a doubt, this was the second. Soon as the words left my mouth, God's response welled up inside of me, *"David, we have been working in three's, now I need you to step out on two (confirmations), because someday I will need you to act immediately when I ask you only once."* He was telling me it was time to grow up, and two confirmations would have to do.

Baltimore was a unique experience. Working in the streets gave me a whole new perspective. I had not realized the amount of poverty and lack that our nation has in its inner cites. I also saw the hope and love that many people are willing to give, even when they have so little. I learned to reach out to anyone and everyone. The trip taught me that all life is precious to God.

Without fail, my new understanding of God was immediately put to a test. As we drove back to Michigan the alternator died just 45 miles from home on a desolate stretch of highway in the middle of the night. There were no visible places to get help, so we just started walking. We discovered a brand new gas station only a half mile away. During the trek I questioned God about why He would allow my car to break down after I had just given Him a week of my life and all the finances to go with it. My heart was stirred at that moment and His Spirit told me God was up to something. Anticipation welled up in me like never before. This was not some chance breakdown; someone in that gas station was in need of a God encounter, and I told David to expect something big.

We found the phone and called for a ride, and then we anxiously waited for God to show up. We bombarded the night cashier with lots of questions but to no avail. Finally, three young people showed up and God went right to work. His Spirit helped David open the door by mentioning God, and then He helped me encourage the group with a couple of my stories. One young man opened up and confessed he was struggling with life and that he needed God to intervene. We prayed right there in that station for God to radically change his life. As we prayed David's sister entered the store and was surprised to see us praying with the young man and his friends. We told her everything we had seen and done in Baltimore and what God had done in that young person's life right there in a small town gas station. He was in God's hands now.

God provided the means to get my car back on the road quickly and inexpensively the next day. There were no tow charges, no labor cost, and I purchased the alternator at a discount. God covered every detail. This was not the kind of trip I would have chosen, but it changed my life forever. I am still reaping the benefits from visiting Baltimore, because I now see people through God's eyes, and I understand the importance of each one of us.

When things appear to go wrong I try to rest in the fact that God is always there to lend a hand. He is looking for people who will help Him reach out to those who are lost and struggling in this world. Instead of worrying about *how* God will get things done, begin living by faith that God *will* finish whatever He starts. God is not looking for talent, just obedience.

During my studies while writing this book I came across this passage.

> *"Everything is permissible"- but not everything is beneficial. "Everything is permissible" – but not everything is constructive. Nobody should see his own good, but the good of others.*

> 1Corinthians 10:23-24 NIV

God wants each of us to live a life full of blessings, but to do that we need to be living in such a way that brings benefits to others as well as ourselves. In truth there are some things we do that have no constructive nature; they serve only self-importance. These actions may be permissible, but they are not truly beneficial to anyone, not even ourselves. However, there are works we can achieve which radically transform the world around us. If we focus on these tasks, we will be able to look back and say that our lives were important, but this will not happen on our own.

> True purpose lies within you. It has been designed into your very existence, but only God can bring it out of you.

Truthfully, we are not perceptive enough to recognize the right tasks. We are blinded too often by our selfish ambitions. We do not know what the world needs. We do not even know what we need. I always thought I needed a bigger house, more money, and more toys to keep the children happy. Then I could give them a life they really deserved because I loved them. When in reality I really needed more patience, more kindness, and more time for my family. The problem was I was just too important to do these things. They were distractions on my way to fulfilling my own selfish desires, even the desires I thought were best for my family. So God got involved in my life, and it has never been the same since. There have been struggles and frustrations along the way, but the benefits sure out weigh the loss. Relationships have been restored, joy has returned, peace is evident in our home, and my heart holds more love than I ever thought imaginable.

True purpose lies within us. It has been designed into our very existence, but only God can bring it out of us. Without God, our lives may still look important, but in the end they will reveal nothing. Importance is our eternal echo; it is what we do in this lifetime that influences the lives of this generation and the generations to come. Purpose has a life of its own. It is as eternal as God himself.

> *Once having been asked by the Pharisees when the kingdom of God would come, Jesus replied, "The kingdom of God does not come by careful observation, nor will people say, 'Here it is,' or 'There it is,' because the kingdom of God is <u>within</u> you."*
> *(emphasis mine)*   Luke 17:20-21 NIV

Your greatest attribute has been encoded into you from the very beginning. To be truly important is to simply reveal God's Spirit working within you.

> *...for it is God who works in you to will and to act according to His good purpose.*
>   Philippians 2:13 NIV

> *For we are God's workmanship, created in Christ Jesus to do good works, which God prepared in advance for us to do.*
>   Ephesians 2:10 NIV

In advance! Everything you need to do is already worked out. Your importance has already been created. By virtue of being here on earth you are already important. Because you exist, you are important. The world is waiting for you to stand up and fulfill your greatest calling, but we cannot use the world's standards to measure our success. This is God's job alone. Mother Theresa passed from this world owning practically nothing, but what she left is still being felt today.

A few years ago I watched a show where a man was investigating lost bank accounts. Each year hundreds of people die without leaving proper information to their heirs. Some had huge amounts of wealth stored up, but they forgot to leave vital information to those they left behind. A life's work totally lost to the family it was intended to bless. You can travel through this life but leave the greatest wealth the world may ever know locked up within you, unspent, untapped, and unnoticed. What is blocking you from seeing God's power working in your life? Whatever it is, give it over to Him, and He will reward you with a much greater treasure: *Purpose!*

I am expecting that God's Spirit will help you find a truth hidden deep within you, one that will impact not only you and your family's life, but my life and the lives of all my children—now and into the future. Stop living in your head and start following your heart, and then you will see the benefits of knowing God.

Task at Hand ✋

1) List all the good qualities you believe God gave you
   that could benefit others.

_____

_____

_____

_____

_____

2) List all the excuses you have for not helping others.

_____

_____

_____

_____

3) List some small things you can start doing today.

_____

_____

_____

_____

_____

NOW STEP OUT!

An abundant life is not one that benefits just us, but one that benefits others as well.

Helpful Biblical Principle:

"Blessed rather are those who hear the word of God and obey it."

Luke 11:28 NIV

Chapter Nine

A New Creation

"Following God means to become someone new."

A New Creation

It is surprising how many people in the church are just waiting around to see the return of Jesus. Someday, Jesus will return in bodily form, but until then we are his ambassadors. Apostle Paul spoke about laboring to form Christ in us. He went on to explain that each of us is a new creation in Christ and old things have passed away (2 Corinthians 5:17). He makes these statements because God's Holy Spirit dwelling in us causes us to be a reflection of Jesus here on earth, just as Jesus was the reflection of the Father during his time on earth. Sure, we may not be perfect all the time, but nevertheless, God desires to show Himself through us. If we would just look and see God's treasure within, we would know Jesus has already returned.

Jesus lived out God's purposes before mankind by listening to his Father's voice and obeying everything he heard through the Holy Spirit. I know that we are frail and open to making mistakes; just look around and you can see our blunders. But if we can keep the eyes fixed upon Jesus and step out into what he shows us, God can still be revealed.

My life has not been glamorous, and each day I have to get up and decide how I will live. Some days I listen closely to what I hear God saying, and other days I get caught up in the busyness of life that quickly drowns out His voice. But every morning I get a new chance to reveal God through my words, my thoughts, and my actions.

This book is a good testament to how easy it is for any of us to get side-tracked in life. I had to wrestle with my American attention span in order to sit down and complete the book God placed on my heart years ago. I believe He had to speak to me years in advance because He knew it would take me that long to get the message. God never got upset. He knew me, and He knew what it would take to get the job done through me. Doing His work does not require perfection on my part, because as I give my commitment He supplies the excellence. God is convinced that our alliance will produce a better me.

> Quit looking for a sign and start being a sign to the world.

The deeper we allow someone into our lives the greater the influence they have on us. All we have to do is to look back at all our past relationships and see how they have changed us, either for better or worse. The power of a real friendship is its ability to change who we are. God understands the value of His companionship and the impact it will have on our lives. He knows that an inward change is necessary if we are to fulfill our true destiny, so each assignment is specifically designed to transform us into His likeness.

When I quit looking for a sign and let God reveal Himself through me, then I started being a sign to everyone around me. There are issues in our lives—there may always be—but it does not sway Him from operating through us. I stopped looking at all my flaws and just started stepping out, God's presence overwhelmed me, and our friendship changed me. Let me share with you a couple of stories to explain my point.

People Are Not This Nice

Most years my boys and I take a trip into the woods of Canada to enjoy a week of camping and fishing. We were making our way home after one of these trips when we spotted a young man walking along the side of the road, so we stopped to see if he needed help. His car had broken down so he hopped in, and as we drove I asked him about his life. He was working a small job, trying to get enough money to go out east to be reunited with his girlfriend and their son. He was concerned that his car was now going to drain his finances and set him back. I could tell by his voice he was discouraged. I began to tell him about how God had been working in our lives and doing amazing things. Not everything worked out the way we wanted, but it was always for the better. He said he once believed more in God, but had kind of gone his own way these last few years.

By the time we reached the next town I had learned a lot about this young man's struggles. I reached under my car seat and gave him a book to encourage him that God would work all these circumstances out for his good. I also tucked the last of my Canadian money in the book to help with his repairs. I told him it was not much, but it was all I had. He looked at me and said, *"People are usually not this nice. You are different than most people who call themselves Christians."*

After we dropped him off, I began to think about his comment. In America you can find a church on almost every corner and with these odds, finding someone who will go out of his or her way to help others should be a lot more common. He was right. Most of us are not willing to be burdened by the needs of others. Our schedules will not allow it, and neither will our budget. We are on a strict timetable to maintain our dreams and goals. But it is time to set our agendas aside and start living like our friend is the King of kings. Random acts of kindness should not be so random in a Christian's life.

Case of the Missing Purse

As I drove through our neighborhood, I noticed a car ahead of me with a large black bag sitting on the trunk. It was one of those situations where the driver was in a hurry and forgot to stow everything inside the vehicle before driving away. The bag fell into the street as the car turned onto the main road. As I got closer and realized what it was, I opened the door, scooped up the purse, and took off in hot pursuit. The car was moving too fast, and finally a red light caused me to lose sight of the vehicle. My new heart demanded that I find the purse's owner and return it, so I did the only thing I knew, I called my friend David. He understood my concept of God and he liked being involved whenever possible.

The moment he answered I told him, "*I have got another WOW story happening right now.*" After a brief explanation he demanded that I drive immediately to his house so that he could be involved. When I arrived at David's house, I realized that I had forgotten to look inside the bag to see what it contained. David quickly stripped the purse from my hands, ripped it open, and dumped out all the contents. Being shy was never a problem for him. What really amazed us was the huge stack of money that fell out—nine hundred dollars in cash, to be exact. That amount of money made this situation even more interesting.

> Jesus put a face on an unseen God, and we put the hands on an unseen Christ.

We went immediately for the wallet to see if we could find a name. The driver had moved, so the address on the license was not current and there was no number listed in the phone book. David made me feel like I was in the presence of a detective. As I was still contemplating our next move, he was already on the phone dialing all the people with the same last name in the phone book. Finally, one voice told us that she was the mother of the owner of the purse. She was aware that her daughter received benefits for her handicapped son during this time of the month, so she is apt to have a lot of extra cash. We agreed that the purse did contain a lot of money and that we just wanted to make sure it was returned to the owner. After a few more phone calls we were in contact with the purse's owner. She was ecstatic, so we set a delivery time and destination.

Upon arrival we were greeted and thanked numerous times for our trouble. What I remember the most was the young lady's brother. He kept repeating, *"People just do not do these kinds of things. They usually take the money and run."* I told him we were not typical people; we were believers, and God wanted us to return this money. We asked if we could pray for them and they agreed. We gathered in a small circle and prayed each one of them. After we parted, David said that what had just transpired was the greatest thing he had ever witnessed, and if anything like that happened again I was required to call him.

An interesting point to this story is that some of David's family did not quite understand his new focus on the supernatural and earlier this particular day David tried to explain his strange behavior to one of his nephews. After we parted David called his nephew right away and told him the entire story. Now he understands how God's involvement can quickly change any situation for the better.

Extravagant Blessings

One of my favorite stories about being a blessing to someone happened outside a restaurant. As my family and I were leaving, a man approached us carrying a take-home container with someone else's half eaten dinner. He told us his finances were depleted and he could not afford to buy groceries, so he was forced to ask for handouts. When he mentioned he had children I knew we needed to help. We could do more than just giving him our leftovers, so I volunteered to take him shopping to get some needed supplies. He agreed to let me buy him some groceries, so I dropped my family off at home, and off we went on our little adventure.

I always prefer to meet a need directly rather than just give money and with my checkbook in hand, I was confident we had enough to buy whatever he wanted. As we walked into the store the gentleman grabbed a basket, but I grabbed a cart. He said he only wanted a few things. When we got to the bread aisle he mentioned that he only wanted one loaf, but I insisted on two. He walked past the fruits and vegetables, so I stopped and asked him what he liked. He said he could not allow me to spend too much money, but I wanted to bless the socks off this guy so I pressed him for more information. After a little prodding, we were soon loaded up on fruits and veggies. He eyed the meat section but tried to avoid it. I caught his glance and steered the cart straight to the cooler. He said that I was spending too much. I explained that it was my money, and I had no problem with it. Each time he pointed something out I grabbed two of them.

By the time we had gone down two isles I heard him say *"You just can't do that"* at least a dozen times, and I noticed tears in his eyes. This man was hoping to only get a few groceries for his daughter, but instead God sent him a stranger who wanted to help out, and no amount of money was too much. I cannot explain how good it felt as we filled the cart and left with a car full of food.

Once we arrived at his house everyone wanted to know what all the commotion was about as we carried in bag after bag. He just grinned and told them that they now had all the food they needed. His smile said it all—God is good. I was truly blessed by what had taken place, and I was extremely grateful that God allowed me to play a small part in that man's life.

> Random acts of kindness should not be so random in a Christian's life.

I never realized that following God was going to be this much fun and so simple. As we give God's Spirit the freedom to guide us, we live according to His standard without even realizing it. I thought it was all about going to church and listening to someone talk. No way—not the God I know. He is involved, outgoing, and anything but boring.

What kind of God are you looking for? So what are you going to do now? Who are you going to be? The world can be a much nicer place if you want it to be. It may cost you a little time and money, but it will be well worth it. Besides, it is God's money anyway, every penny of it.

Task at Hand ✋

<u>First</u>, write down the nicest thing you ever did for somebody and how it made you feel.

_____

_____

_____

_____

_____

<u>Second</u>, ask God to make you better giver.

"Father, Give me the compassion to see the needs in others around me, the resources to provide assistance, the courage to lend a helping hand, and the heart to do everything in love. I ask this in Jesus' name. Amen."

<u>Third</u>, ask God to give you more chances to give to the people around you this week and write them down.

- Chances I Had To Give This Week -

_____

_____

_____

_____

_____

_____

We are the hands, feet, and mouth of a loving, unseen God. Reveal the Christ in you!

Helpful Biblical Principles

For God is working in you, giving you the desire to obey him and the power to do what pleases him.

Philippians 2:13 NLT

- *Chapter Ten* -

The Kingdom

"Living a supernatural life"

Being supernatural should be as normal as breathing when you belong to God, but to experience that kind of life you must first believe that it actually exists. The kingdom of God is an unseen realm that is actually impacting and altering the natural world around us. If you are willing to discover its authenticity you must live by faith. Jesus' faith brought heaven to earth when he spoke to the wind and the water to calm the storm (Luke 8:24). He understood this when he taught us to pray, "...*your kingdom come your will be done on earth as it is in heaven...*" (Matthew 6:9). God answered that prayer by allowing us to access every provision in heaven and establish them here on earth. He accomplished this through the works of Jesus. This means that each of us should be living in peace, joy, and health, because nothing has been withheld from us.

In an effort to discover why my circumstances fell short of that abundant life, I was forced to look deeper into myself. My search revealed that I held some assumptions about God which fit my lifestyle, but in essence were hindering me from knowing the whole truth. Inspiring preachers, powerful messages, and insightful books filled with great wisdom were not releasing God's full power glory into my life. My current beliefs or theology about God were holding me back, so the time came for me to find out what God believed. I needed to separate fact from fiction. There was only one person who knew the true meaning behind the Bible, and that was the person who inspired it: God, Himself. Since everything else was just an opinion, I decided to take all my questions to Him and see what He had to say. He began to use His signs to teach me that there was more going on around me than I could see or understand.

I now understand why some people did not want to hear Jesus' version of God: it was because they had already decided to trust only what their fathers and church fellowship believed. There was no place for new truth in their reasoning and logic. The disciples, on the other hand, decided to let go of long-held beliefs and to follow a man who spoke something radically new. At one point, almost every follower deserted Jesus because his words were too tough, and when he asked the final twelve disciples why they stayed, Peter replied, *"Lord, to whom shall we go? You have the words of eternal life."* (John 6:68) They found a new truth, and they were willing to abandon over six hundred years of the Hebrew law to accept Jesus as the Messiah. They upgraded their theology through experience.

> There is nothing stronger than God's power, except the rules we keep Him under.

Are you willing to put your beliefs to the test and change them if necessary?

I want to share a few stories of how God put our family's beliefs to the test. The farther we were willing to go, the greater God became. As we discovered new truths, we discovered God was bigger than we had imagined. Actually, God was not getting bigger (He has always been infinitely big) *we* were.

Most of us believe our words are merely sounds that simply convey ideas to one another. Yet, our lives are a direct result of the creative nature released by the words we speak, both positive and negative. Any words, spoken by faith, carry a supernatural power that gives us the ability to prevail over any difficulty we may encounter. The following miracle opened our eyes to power of God's authority here on earth.

Can You Hear Me Now

At this point in my life I was spending numerous hours working outside the home trying to make extra money. I had been gone most of the day, and when I returned home that evening, I found out that this was what had transpired...

Joshua was twelve at the time, and our family was getting ready for a trip to the barber shop. My wife was focusing her attention on preparing the girls while the boys got themselves ready. Geralynn gave our daughter Katelynn a cotton swab to keep her occupied while she cleaned her ears. Katelynn was eager to put her cotton swab to work so she asked Joshua if she could clean his ears and being a good older brother, he agreed. The only thing

Geralynn remembered was hearing a loud shriek just before Joshua came running into the bathroom with blood dripping from his ear. Katelynn had forced her cotton swab deep into his ear causing considerable damage.

In the heat of the moment Geralynn remembered that we knew the name of Jesus had stopped bleeding before, so without hesitation she placed her hand on his ear and commanded it to stop bleeding. In an instant the bleeding stopped. Joshua, however, was still in great pain and could not hear from his damaged ear, so Geralynn told him to ask God if they should go to the hospital or go get their haircuts. This was merely a ploy to allow her a few moments to get the other children ready for an immediate trip to the emergency room.

Joshua went into the bedroom and began repeating the phrase, *"In Jesus' name I will hear, In Jesus' name I will hear ..."* After preparing everyone to leave Geralynn asked Joshua what God wanted him to do. *"Mom, it (sound) just came back on and my ear still kind of hurts, but God said we should just get our hair cut, everything is all right."*

I wanted to know what the doctor said and was shocked when I learned they never went to the hospital. We had never relied totally on God before when it came to the children, but Geralynn was at peace with the decision. I inquired why she did not go anyway, and she said that Joshua was so fully convinced that everything was all right that she knew she could trust his decision.

We monitored his ear to make sure everything was working properly. A couple of days later while carefully cleaning his ear to remove some bloody debris, a good sized chunk of material fell into the sink. It was big enough to clog the entire ear canal and stop any sound from reaching the ear drum. We do not know how Joshua even could have even heard any sound with that much stuff in his ear. Miraculously, God was allowing him hear, and today his hearing is still perfect. It was when we spoke to our situation that God's power manifested and we got to experience His work once again. I also knew why Geralynn was the one home that day and not me. She had the faith to believe Joshua's trust in God's healing power. I probably would have demanded we go the hospital route. With Joshua healthy and hearing fine, I was able to believe God helped us once again. God's grace over our lives was getting more noticeable day by day. Even our children were beginning to see Him, as Katelynn taught us in the next story.

Personal Escort

One cool, Fall day we were scurrying about the house trying to put things in order for a small church meeting in our home when the doorbell rang. It was too early for our church visitors to arrive, and when I opened the door I was greeted by two nervous young girls. They were eager to come inside, and upon entering they asked to use our phone. When I asked if everything was all right, they informed us of their situation.

The girls had skipped school with some boys

earlier in the day and ended up at a house in an unfamiliar neighborhood. The young ladies felt uneasy when more boys arrived. The situation took a turn for the worse, so the girls snuck out the back door and ran aimlessly throughout the neighborhood in an attempt to elude any followers. They ran until they felt safe, and then began to look for a place to use the phone.

They were still afraid that some of the boys may have followed them, so as they called home I watched for any unfamiliar faces roaming the block. After several calls to friends and family the girls were unable to contact anyone. It took a few minutes, but we got them to calm down, and assured them we would see to it they got home safely. Geralynn approached me and said she felt she was supposed to take them home. They lived across town, and she would be late for our home study, but we agreed it was the best thing to do.

Once we informed the girls that we would provide transportation home, one young lady told us that as they were running down the block they noticed that our house glowed. *"It was brighter than the other houses," she said, "and I felt like we were supposed to come to your house to use the phone because we knew it was a safe place."* God had sent them to us for safe keeping, so that was what we intended to do.

Geralynn drove the girls home, while I got ready for the meeting. When Geralynn arrived home thirty minutes later she had a very amazing story. Our daughter, Katelynn, who was three at the time, went along for the ride. During their drive Katelynn kept sliding as far forward in her seat as possible trying to look out the front window. This made Geralynn uncomfortable so she requested she sit back, but Katelynn ignored any attempts to keep her properly seated. Geralynn inquired into what was capturing her attention. Katelynn replied, *"Don't you see Him, mama?"* *"See who?"* My wife asked. *"Jesus"*, Katelynn responded, and then added, *"Right up there above the trees. He is moving along with us and He stops when we stop. Can you see Him?"* Geralynn said Katelynn kept pointing and commenting the entire trip about actually seeing Jesus following the car. It brought the scripture to light. *Where two or more come together in my name, there I am among them* (Matthew 18:20). We agreed God wanted us to help get these young girls home safely, and we believe He personally kept us safe in the process. We were actually experiencing God in away we never dreamed of.

The stuff I was reading about in the Bible was making more sense, and I was actually getting to see it in action. Unfortunately, many of the other Christians I spoke to have never had these types of experiences. Somehow we have sterilized God's word, not on purpose, but it has made it unproductive. Powerless lifestyles are a direct result of trying to keep God within our realm of understanding, traditions, and religion.

Does your God heal the sick? Does He still perform miraculous sign and wonders? Is He willing to speak to you? Does your God have the power to change your life, or are your circumstances beyond

His control? You need to ask yourself these questions and take a good look at what you believe.

As Christians, we have limited God's power by making it fit the rules we have been taught about what He can and cannot do. God's word is living and active (Hebrews 4:12), so its primary purpose is to enter our minds and hearts and begin changing what we believe about Him. Without a God-experience, many in the church today have become trapped in a lifeless set of rules. Paul warned Timothy that in the latter days of the church many people would have a form of godliness but would deny it had any power to influence their lives (2 Timothy 3:5). That is sterilization. As for me, I wanted all God had to offer, even if I had to let go of everything I trusted in the past. Each day God helps me take another small step of faith in His direction, and one day He showed me how far I had come.

> To live with God means to learn to live without limits.

Shaky Ground

I had just entered the building and was about to start what I thought would be just another ordinary day of work when I felt the ground tremble. The shaking felt like vibrations you encounter when heavy equipment is pounding on the ground, and there was new construction happening at the other end of the building. I noticed the vibrations all the way down the hall, and they were strangely in time with each step I took. Whenever I paused the vibrations ceased. From my office window, I could see no equipment that would have created these vibrations. A stroll past the construction site revealed no large machinery at all. I pondered that situation and decided I needed to ask God if He knew anything.

To my surprise God had orchestrated the entire event. He spoke to my heart, *"You are feeling in the natural what you are in the spirit."* He explained further that every time I entered my job I was sending out spiritual waves (vibrations) to all the unseen forces letting them know I was there acting on behalf of Jesus Christ. It was as if all the spiritual forces knew that Jesus had entered the building.

That day I realized that we are Christ's representatives here on earth (2 Corinthians 5:20). When we allow God to work through us, it is as if He is here, and everything around us senses His vibrations coming from our lives. As I now begin my day, I try to set my mind and heart on God's desires. Some days I may encourage others to increase their faith, or I may pray for someone's difficult circumstances, or I may just show a small gesture of kindness, but whatever I do, I try to do it for the sake of Christ. When my life is focused on God's direction, His presence is quite noticeable. I cannot even begin to count the number of times He has touched the lives around me, and it is comforting to be a part in His grand scheme.

Before another example of how the heavenly realm made its way into the natural, I want to talk about a community of people known as the *"Bereans"* (Acts 17). They were specifically identified as being *"more noble than the rest"* because they typically searched to see if what Apostle Paul taught was true. A noble person would not run to a book or a specific group of people just to prove someone or something wrong, so I made up my mind that I would only search for truth, God's truth. Theology was about to take a back seat.

Native Tongues

When my mother was a young believer, there was great debate about speaking in tongues. She did not know what to believe, but during a prayer for the gift of the Holy Spirit she began to mutter in a strange manner. The Bible calls it speaking in tongues. Mom went home and sought the Lord. She wanted to know if this was truly a gift from God. She asked for a sign or a confirmation. Later mom received a dream where God spoke to her and called her "*authentic.*" She awoke and asked the Lord to authenticate His gifts. What happened next proved to her that this actually was a gift from God.

Mom was working as a registered nurse in a nursing home. There was one particular patient who spoke only broken English, and the nursing staff found her difficult to work with. One evening while Mom was attending to the lady, God placed it on her heart to pray with her. After a few moments of relaying the idea she was agreeable to the request. During mom's prayer, the Lord interrupted and asked her to pray in the new spiritual language she had received at the service. Mom gave in with only a quiet prayer. The Lord directed her to pray loud enough for the lady to hear her gift of tongues. Mom gave in again, and as she prayed she noted a definite change in the women's expressions. When Mom finished, the lady looked at her and said, *"You are the first person to speak to me in my native language in forty years."* Then she got out of bed, hugged my mom, and in her best English she said, *"I know you justa love me."*

From that day on, the lady's personality changed dramatically, and the entire staff noticed the difference. The nurses asked my Mom what had happened on her shift, but she told them that they would not understand. At that moment Mom knew this was a gift from God and not just any gift, but an authentic one!

> If you think God is not able to change your life, then maybe it is time to believe something different.

Our family experienced the same gift years later. As my boys were growing up, we attended the same church I attended as a small boy. The family was growing and moving forward in God's graces while I was learning to hear from God and act on whatever He told me. It was Sunday, and the boys were getting ready for a special service at church. They were about to take part in a service that we were taught would propel them to a new level of faith. We believed that the Holy Spirit would fill them with a greater baptism than before. As we were getting ready, the Lord kept speaking to me that it was my place as their father to bestow this powerful gift upon my sons, just as God, my Father, had bestowed the gift of the Holy Spirit upon me. I spoke with my wife, and explained what God was putting on my heart. She was in full agreement that we should be the ones to release this gift to our boys.

As we gathered in the bathroom and prayed over our boys to receive God's Holy Spirit, each one raised his arms and began to speak in tongues. We were all amazed and greatly encouraged that God is still releasing His gifts today.

Let us close with a prayer:

"Father, you are the creator of heaven and earth. I am your creation, and there is more in this world than I may fully understand. Today, I ask you to open my heart to accept more of you. Change me on the inside and give me a teachable spirit so I may see the truth of who you really are. In Jesus' name. Amen."

Task at Hand

Pray for God to supernaturally touch the lives of some of your family and close friends. Pray for specific things and ask God to let you see the results of your prayers.

Note: Pray every day until something happens. It may help to write it on an index card and place it in an obvious place, like on the bathroom mirror or the dashboard of your car.

Prayer_____

_____

_____

Signs_____

_____

_____

Prayer_____

_____

_____

Signs_____

_____

_____

(Repeat as often as possible)

In life
you have to
take risks
if you want
to encounter the
Kingdom of God
and find
your true
destiny.

Helpful Biblical Principle

I will instruct you (says the Lord) and guide you along the best pathway for your life; I will advise you and watch your progress.

Psalm 32:8 TLB

Chapter Eleven

A Final Note

"The world is waiting for us"

A Final Note

If we want to become our best we must establish quality friendships. We need to have people in our lives that are free to tell us the truth about ourselves. God is the type of friend who is determined to bring out the best in us. His voice speaks to our potential and His works are designed to strengthen our limitations.

God loves us the way we are, but He refuses to let us stay that way. He created us with a purpose, and an encounter with His kindness propels us to live a new life; a better life. Whether you are a servant or a king you have not reached your full potential until God's presence fills your entire being. Once you encounter God's grace and understand who He really is, you become a sign that encourages others to look deeper into the things of God. The people we touch then reach out for their own experiences and in turn reach out to someone else. The woman at the well shows us how this principle works.

Woman at the Well

Jacob's well was there, and Jesus, tired as he was from the journey, sat down by the well. It was about the sixth hour. When a Samaritan woman came to draw water, Jesus said to her, "Will you give me a drink?" (His disciples had gone into the town to buy food.) The Samaritan woman said to him, "You are a Jew and I am a Samaritan woman. How can you ask me for a drink?" (For Jews do not associate with Samaritans.) Jesus answered her, "If you knew the gift of God and who it is that asks you for a drink, you would have asked him and he would have given you living water." "Sir," the woman said, "you have nothing to draw with and the well is deep. Where can you get this living water?... Jesus answered, "Everyone who drinks this water will be thirsty again, but whoever drinks the water I give him will never thirst. Indeed, the water I give him will become in him a spring of water welling up to eternal life." The woman said to him, "Sir, give me this water so that I won't get thirsty and have to keep coming here to draw water." He told her, "Go, call your husband and come back." "I have no husband," she replied. Jesus said to her, "You are right when you say you have no husband. The fact is, you have had five husbands, and the man you now have is not your husband. What you have just said is quite true."... The woman said, "I know that the Messiah" (called Christ) "is coming. When he comes, he will explain everything to us."

Then Jesus declared, "I who speak to you am he." Just then his disciples returned and were surprised to find him talking with a woman. But no one asked, "What do you want?" or "Why are you talking with her?" Then, leaving her water jar, the woman went back to the town and said to the people, "Come, see a man who told me everything I ever did. Could this be the Christ?" They came out of the town and made their way toward him... Many of the Samaritans from that town believed in him because of the woman's testimony, "He told me everything I ever did." So when the Samaritans came to him, they urged him to stay with them, and he stayed two days. And because of his words many more became believers. They said to the woman, "We no longer believe just because of what you said; now we have heard for ourselves, and we know that this man really is the Savior of the world."

(... means, Author removed verses to clarify)

John 4:6-42 NIV

The woman at the well encountered Jesus as she went about her daily routine. She was not living a devout Christian life, she was just being herself. Jesus knew everything about her life, the good and the bad, but it did not prevent him from showing her compassion and grace. In fact, despite her circumstances Jesus offered his greatest gift, acceptance. There is no lifestyle that can keep God away, His love for you compels Him to seek you out. At this very moment, God is reaching out and waiting for you to accept His friendship. It is a gift freely given from the Creator of the Universe. Our alliance with God provides us with complete access to His never-ending kindness, infinite grace, limitless mercy and unfailing love, so claim what is rightfully yours today.

The woman at the well was willing to accept what Jesus was offering and she shared her experience with those in her town. Her encouragement created a desire in the others to seek out Jesus and develop their own faith in Christ. Those personal experiences ground us in the fact that God is real. I hope my stories encouraged you, but the truth is you need your own experiences. No matter what you believe or what you hear, never give up on your search for God. He is your greatest reward.

Task at Hand

Let us see how far you have come in your journey.

(1-100%)

I believe in God   _____%

I know God hears me   _____%

I expect God to answer my prayers   _____%

I can recognize God speaking to me   _____%

I know God wants to be my friend   _____%

It is time to move forward!

Blessings, on your travels with my friend.

Jesus'
presence
in our lives
make us
completely
innocent
and
totally
acceptable
in God eyes.

Our job
is to start living
like its true,
today!

Helpful Biblical Principle:

How we praise God, the Father of our Lord Jesus Christ, who has blessed us with every spiritual blessing in the heavenly realms because we belong to Christ. Long ago, even before he made the world, God loved us and chose us in Christ to be holy and without fault in his eyes. His unchanging plan has always been to adopt us into his own family by bringing us to himself through Jesus Christ. And this gave him great pleasure. So we praise God for the wonderful kindness he has poured out on us because we belong to his dearly loved Son. He is so rich in kindness that he purchased our freedom through the blood of his Son, and our sins are forgiven. He has showered his kindness on us, along with all wisdom and understanding. God's secret plan has now been revealed to us; it is a plan centered on Christ, designed long ago according to his good pleasure.

Ephesians 1:3-10 NLT

Epilogue

Prayers listed in the book.

Prayer for a commitment to God...

God, forgive me for all my sins and mistakes. Take over my life and help me live the life you desire. I accept your forgiveness in Jesus' name. Amen.

Request for a personal God experience...

God reveal yourself to me in some way so that I know you exist. Make it obvious to me and help me to see what you are doing. I ask this in Jesus' name.

Prayer for an increase of God's Spirit...

Father I ask for more of your Holy Spirit to fill me and guide me. Immerse me into your powerful Spirit and reveal all there is about you. I ask this in the name of Jesus Christ, your son.

Prayer to hear God's voice...

Father, speak to me in a way that I can understand your voice. Give me the eyes to see and the ears to hear what you are saying. I ask for your guidance in Jesus' name.

Prayer for the renewing of your heart...

Lord, I do not know you as well as I should. I ask that you reveal your love and commitment to me in a powerful way. Open up my heart to receive the faith that you exist and the courage to follow your call. In Jesus' name. Amen.

Prayer for faith in the time of doubt...

Father, you said you would never leave me nor forsake me, but sometimes I struggle with the idea that all circumstances are designed for my good. Speak to me in a way I will understand. Give me the eyes to see you working and the ears to hear your leading. I ask this in the name of your son, Jesus.

Prayer to step out as God's ambassador...

Father, Give me the compassion to see the needs in others around me, the resources to provide assistance, the courage to lend a helping hand, and the heart to do everything in love. I ask this in Jesus' name. Amen.

Prayer to believe beyond your current faith...

Father, you are the creator of heaven and earth. I am your creation, and there is more in this world than I may fully understand. Today, I ask you to open my heart to accept more of you. Change me on the inside and give me a teachable spirit so I may see the truth of who you really are. In Jesus' name. Amen.

– NOTES –

Chapter 2
1. Merlin R. Carothers, *Prison to Praise*, (Merlin R. Carothers, 1970) ISBN 0-943026-02-4

God speaks to our potential, not our present condition. Gideon was hiding from the enemy in a winepress when God showed up and called him "A might man of valor". He had to go to battle with God to discover his true calling. You need to know who you are and what motivates you. Otherwise, you may not understand what God sees in you. Below I have listed two references below that are designed to help you discover what is in your heart.

1. Florence Littauer, *Personality Plus* (Baker Book House Company, 2002).

2. Mark Gungor, *Discovering Your Heart with the Flag Page* (Laugh Your Way America LLC, 2007).   www.flagpagetest.com

Quick Order Form

_____
Name

_____
Address

_____
City, State, Zip

(_____) _____
　Telephone

_____
Email address (optional)

Costs:
(1-4 books)　　　　$12.99ea + 1.00 shipping　Total ($13.99)us
(Set of 5 books)　$54.95 + 3.00 shipping　　Total ($57.95)us
　　　　　　　　($10.99 per book, Savings of $10)
(Set of 10 books)　$99.90 + 5.00 shipping　　Total ($104.90)us
　　　　　　　　($9.99 per book, Savings of $30)

Books ordered _____ _____ _____ _____
　　　　　　　　Individual　Set of 5　Set of 10　Total Books

Total Cost with shipping: _____
　　　Please contact us for International orders- send no money

Please send Check or money orders only, payable to
"Winding Road Ministries"

Internet orders:
　　　　　www.windingroadministries.com
Mail orders:
　　　　　Winding Road Ministries
　　　　　P.O. Box 155
　　　　　Eaton Rapids, Michigan 48827-0155

Information about Winding Road Ministries,
David Jackson or Speaking/Seminars send to the
address above or email us at
office@windingroadministries.com

Quick Order Form

_____
Name

_____
Address

_____
City, State, Zip

(_____) _____
Telephone

_____
Email address (optional)

Costs:
(1-4 books) $12.99ea + 1.00 shipping   Total ($13.99)us
(Set of 5 books) $54.95 + 3.00 shipping   Total ($57.95)us
                   ($10.99 per book, Savings of $10)
(Set of 10 books) $99.90 + 5.00 shipping   Total ($104.90)us
                   ($9.99 per book, Savings of $30)

Books ordered _____   _____   _____   _____
              Individual   Set of 5   Set of 10   Total Books

Total Cost with shipping: _____
      Please contact us for International orders- send no money

Please send Check or money orders only, payable to
"Winding Road Ministries"

Internet orders:
            www.windingroadministries.com
Mail orders:
            Winding Road Ministries
            P.O. Box 155
            Eaton Rapids, Michigan 48827-0155

Information about Winding Road Ministries,
David Jackson or Speaking/Seminars send to the
address above or email us at
office@windingroadministries.com